AFRICA, YOU HAVE A FRIEND IN WASHINGTON

ADST MEMOIRS AND OCCASIONAL PAPERS SERIES
Series Editors: Lisa Terry & Margery Thompson

In 2003, the Association for Diplomatic Studies and Training (ADST), a non-profit organization founded in 1986, created the Memoirs and Occasional Papers Series to preserve firsthand accounts and other informed observations on foreign affairs for scholars, journalists, and the general public. Through its book series, its Foreign Affairs Oral History program, and its support for the training of foreign affairs personnel at the State Department's Foreign Service Institute, ADST seeks to promote understanding of American diplomacy and those who conduct it. Former ambassador and assistant secretary for African Affairs Herman J. "Hank" Cohen has given us the concise memoirs of the State Department's "Mr. Africa."

RELATED TITLES IN ADST SERIES

Claudia E. Anyaso, *Fifty Years of U.S. Africa Policy: Reflections of Assistant Secretaries for African Affairs and U.S. Embassy Officials*

Herman J. Cohen, *Intervening in Africa: Superpower Peacemaking in a Troubled Continent*

———, *The Mind of the African Strongman: Conversations with Dictators, Statesmen, and Father Figures*

———, *U.S. Policy Toward Africa: Eight Decades of Realpolitik*

Harriet Elam-Thomas, *Diversifying Diplomacy: My Journey from Roxbury to Dakar*

Robert E. Gribbin, *In the Aftermath of Genocide: The U.S. Role in Rwanda*

Brandon Grove, *Behind Embassy Walls: The Life and Times of an American Diplomat*

Michael P. E. Hoyt, *Captive in the Congo: A Consul's Return to the Heart of Darkness*

Edmund J. Hull, *High-Value Target: Countering al Qaeda in Yemen*

Cameron Hume, *Mission to Algiers: Diplomacy by Engagement*

Robert H. Miller, *Vietnam and Beyond: A Diplomat's Cold War Education*

David D. Newsom, *Witness to a Changing World*

Richard B. Parker, *Uncle Sam in Barbary: A Diplomatic History*

———, *Memoirs of a Foreign Service Arabist*

Raymond F. Smith, *The Craft of Political Analysis for Diplomats*

James W. Spain, *In Those Days: A Diplomat Remembers*

William G. Thom, *African Wars: Recollections of a Defense Intelligence Officer*

Jean Wilkowski, *Abroad for Her Country: Tales of a Pioneer Woman Ambassador in the U.S. Foreign Service*

For a complete list of series titles, visit <adst.org/publications>

AFRICA, YOU HAVE A FRIEND IN WASHINGTON

An American Diplomat's Adventures
South of the Sahara

HERMAN J. COHEN

Association for Diplomatic Studies and Training
Memoirs and Occasional Papers Series

NEW ACADEMIA PUBLISHING
VELLUM

Washington, DC

Library of Congress Control Number: 2023905903
ISBN 979-8-9875893-4-2 paperback (alk. paper)

VELLUM An imprint of New Academia Publishing

NEW ACADEMIA
PUBLISHING

New Academia Publishing
4401-A Connecticut Ave. NW, #236, Washington DC 20008
info@newacademia.com - www.newacademia.com

To my spouse Suzanne, my late son Marc, my son Alain, my daughter-in-law Lauren, and my three grandchildren, Gabriella, Valentina, and Alain II

Contents

List of Illustrations

All are U.S. Department of State photos in the public domain and include the author

Prologue

New York Youth

I spent most of my early youth in a New York neighborhood populated mainly by immigrant families. Virtually all the adults I knew were born outside of the United States, including my own parents. My mother came from Latvia, my father from Lithuania. My classmates had parents who came from a variety of countries, including Romania, Hungary, Austria, Italy, and China. Hearing foreign languages and foreign accents gave me a strong interest in the world outside the United States.

In 1942, when I was ten years old, my older brother went into the United States Army at the start of the Second World War. I took a keen interest in his travels, from Louisiana, to Brazil, Ghana, Egypt, India, and Burma. Before he departed, he gave me his stamp collection, with issues from fifty-four countries. In elementary school, my teachers asked us to copy maps of Latin America and Africa.

In Thomas Jefferson High School, in the East New York Section of Brooklyn, I was fortunate to be selected for the honors program during my junior and senior years. That program provided for advanced research and oral presentations. My thesis topic was a comparison of economic planning in Brazil and India. During my oral presentation, I faced tough questioning from my fellow students.

At the City College of New York, I took an interest in journalism. I worked for the student newspaper, becoming the editor-in-chief in my junior year. With that experience, I decided that I wanted to become a foreign correspondent. During my required military service, the U.S. Army sent me to West Germany, which afforded me the opportunity to visit most of Western Europe. These experiences further whetted my appetite for all things foreign.

After my army service, I had a choice between two opportunities—pursuing a graduate degree at the Harvard School of Business or entering the Foreign Service. The State Department told me that I could delay my entry into the Foreign Service in order to do the Harvard degree. But I was impatient to start working and decided on immediate entry into the Foreign Service.

In 1955 during my first month in the Foreign Service, I took note of the fact that the British and French governments were preparing their African colonies for independence. I decided to try to get in on the ground floor of U.S. diplomacy in Africa. I remember inquiring about the Africa Bureau. I was informed that the "Africa Bureau" consisted of two Foreign Service officers, Jerry Lavalee and Fritz Picard, who were sharing an office in the Middle East Bureau. When I went to see them, they were delighted to welcome me to diplomacy in Africa.

In 1956, the State Department established an actual Africa Bureau to start organizing American embassies in thirty-five about-to-be-independent African nations. I decided at that point to become a specialist in African affairs.

My first foreign assignment was to Paris, where I was sent to improve my French language capability, since I had failed to pass the required examination. It was only after that assignment that I was able to set my sights on specializing in African affairs. In 1962, I was assigned to the East African nation of Uganda. My African specialization had begun.

1

INTERNATIONAL SERVICE BECKONS

"Hank, have you considered taking the entrance examination for the Foreign Service?" The question was posed by Professor Bernard E. Brown at the City College of New York, where I earned my undergraduate degree.

It was the Fall semester of 1951 during which I had done the impossible. I took both of Professor Brown's courses in international relations in a single semester, and I received a grade of A in both. In addition to being known as a tough grader, Brown also assigned a heavy reading load, with a requirement for knowledgeable class discussion.

My response to Professor Brown was, "I have not given it any thought. Besides, it is well known that the Foreign Service is reserved for Ivy League graduates. But, since you raised the issue, I might give it a try."

I sat for the examination in the Fall of 1951. It was a three-day affair, mornings and afternoons, and included a combination of multiple-choice and essay questions. For each essay, we were instructed to write no more than a maximum number of words. At the end of the essay, we were required to indicate the number of words written. Needless to say, we were all exhausted at the end of the third day.

The results came in during the Spring of 1953. The passing grade was 70. I had earned a 72. I was told to be ready to be invited for the oral examination. Before I could do that, however, I would be required to spend two years in the U.S. military. I had participated in the full four-year Reserve Officers' Training Corps at City College and was therefore entitled to enter the U.S. Army as a second lieutenant.

I completed the basic officer course at the U.S. Army Infantry Training School at Fort Benning, Georgia. The army then assigned me to Germany as an infantry platoon leader in the 43rd Armored Infantry Battalion of the Second Armored Division, located near the town of Baumholder in the Rhine region. Since the post–World War II allied occupation of Germany was still in force in 1953, our division was officially a guest in the French zone.

During my first year with the 43rd, I spent a lot of time on maneuvers. I had the impression that our heavy vehicles were ploughing up a lot of farmlands and destroying a lot of crops. When I expressed my dismay, I was informed that the farmers were receiving cash compensation.

After the first year, the army transferred me to division headquarters in the town of Bad Kreuznach, also in the French zone. In contrast to austere and colorless Baumholder, Bad Kreuznach was a delightful spa resort on the Nahe river, where people with aches and pains came to take the rich mineral waters. Why was I assigned there? The new division commander, a major general, found that, in the French zone, most of the officials he had to deal with were French, both civilian and military. He wanted someone near him who could interpret for him and who could deal directly with the French personnel.

During my first month in Bad Kreuznach, I decided one Friday evening to participate in a Jewish sabbath service at the base chapel. While there, I noted the presence of a Frenchman, who introduced himself as Pierre Engel, a French diplomat serving as governor of the district. Over the next few weeks, we became good friends, thereby considerably facilitating my responsibility for liaison with the French authorities on behalf of the commanding general.

During that second year in Germany, I took advantage of half-fare travel on the German railway system available to occupying forces. I traveled to France, the United Kingdom, Austria, and the Netherlands. This travel, as well as my time in Germany, heightened my interest in international relations. I began to relish the challenge of analyzing foreign cultures and their political systems. I decided to continue pursuing a career in international service of some sort, journalism, business, or the U.S. government.

I was reminded of my pending application for the U.S. Foreign

Service when I received an order to report to the U.S. Consulate General in Frankfurt for a security interview. Frankfurt was about an hour away from Bad Kreuznach by train.

I arrived at the Consulate General in full dress uniform, which resulted in the U.S. Marine guards' saluting and clicking their heels as I walked past them. It was great for my ego. The interview was routine. I was told that the oral interview part of the exam would take place as soon as I returned to Washington.

I was discharged from the military when I returned to the United States in April 1955. The next month, I traveled to Washington for the oral examination.

There I met with three retired Foreign Service officers, who, unlike today, had no prepared script. They looked at my biography and asked whatever questions came to mind. Their objective seemed to be to determine how "American" I was. I had questions about major league baseball and U.S. politics. They also asked questions about foreign governments.

For example, I was asked to compare the British Labour and Conservative parties. I discussed both for a few minutes and then said that the two parties were essentially the same, with one being in power and the other out of power. This caused an argument within the examining panel that continued for a few minutes while I watched. Fortunately, it all turned out fine, and they told me I had been accepted. I would be notified when to start the entering officers' course at the Foreign Service Institute. This was May 1955, and I was sworn into the Foreign Service in July 1955.

One of the basic requirements for tenure in the U.S. Foreign Service is fluency in a foreign language. I had studied French in high school and college. To find my level, I took the State Department French examination. On a scale of 1 to 5, the passing grade is 3. My score was 2. Because I flunked, I was given intensive French training every afternoon, with training tapes for the evenings.

My first assignment was to the American Embassy in Paris as a visa-issuing officer. I took the French examination one more time before embarking for Paris and was still not successful, with a score of 2+. I arrived in Paris in October 1955 under probation. I needed to pass the French examination within one year or I would have to leave the Service.

2

PARIS TEN YEARS AFTER WORLD WAR II

The American Embassy in Paris is one of the largest U.S. diplomatic missions in the world. In the language of bureaucracy, it is listed as Class One, on a scale of one to four. It is located on Avenue Gabriel, just off the famous Place de la Concorde in city center. The main building dates from decades before World War II and proudly displays bullet holes from a few days of combat.

Because of the many U.S. government agencies that maintain offices in Paris, the embassy is located in a number of buildings in separate neighborhoods. I was assigned to the Visa Section, located across Avenue Gabriel from the main Chancery. The two-story building shared space with the office of the Marshall Plan, which was in process of phasing out in 1955.

The Visa Section had five American officers, including a consul in charge and four vice consuls. Two officers were assigned to visa issuance for both visitors and immigrants. One officer was in charge of Refugee Relief, a Europe-wide program designed to re-settle displaced persons. I was surprised to learn that there were still displaced persons ten years after the end of the war. The fourth officer dealt with difficult cases involving applicants who might be considered ineligible to go to the United States for a long list of reasons, which are listed in the Immigration and Nationality Act of 1952.

In addition to the American officers, there were seven French employees who played a key role in the basic processing of applications. In the U.S. diplomatic system, citizens of the local government are known as Foreign Service Nationals, or FSNs. In 1955, there were a few aging veterans who had joined the embassy prior to World War II. They proudly informed me that they continued to receive their American salaries throughout the war via the Swiss embassy.

I was assigned as one of the two regular visa issuing officers. In 1955, we interviewed approximately fifty applicants daily. In the year 2019, the number of travelers to the United States from France was in the tens of thousands. Needless to say, the 1955 system involving a personal interview for each applicant could not last.

The persons receiving visitor visas in 1955 were mainly business travelers, with only a minimum number of tourists. Hardly a day passed without one or two visa applicants of special interest. For example, I issued a visa to Audrey Hepburn, the Hollywood star who was traveling with a Dutch passport.

One day, I noted the FSNs buzzing about a V.I.P. who was expected. It turned out to be the president of Kodak France. When the gentleman arrived, I opened his passport and saw the name Prince Murat. Here was a descendant of one of Napoleon's top generals.

About half of the daily visa issuance was for immigrants heading for permanent residency in the United States. I noted that a large percentage of the French persons seeking immigration were from Brittany. Some of them told me that their plan was to work in the United States and save money so that they could return to Brittany and build large homes.

While most of the work of visa issuance was routine, there were moments of drama. During the summer of 1956, for instance, I was summoned to the office of the U.S. ambassador to France. As one of the most junior diplomats in the Foreign Service, I wondered why. There, I met the political counselor, Walter Stoessel, who was number three in the hierarchy.

Stoessel told me that the embassy was facing a major public relations problem. The highly popular and successful French movie star and cabaret singer, Yves Montand, had signed a contract to go to Hollywood to costar in a film with Marilyn Monroe. So, what was the problem?

Yves Montand was an open and proud member of the French Communist Party. There were several celebrities in that category. It was fashionable. The problem was that the Immigration and Nationality Act prohibited the issuance of visas to members of the

Communist Party. In order for Yves Montand to be able to travel to Hollywood, we were required to request a special waiver that would allow him to make a single visit. Stoessel's message to me was that I needed to make a very persuasive request for a waiver. Washington was still under the influence of McCarthyism, and the approval of a waiver would not be automatic. If a waiver were not approved, and Montand could not go to Hollywood, we would be heavily criticized, and laughed at, by the French press.

I proceeded to write the waiver request, emphasizing the overall cultural and political interests of the United States in France. I took two days to develop my arguments. I sent it to Washington. Two weeks later, in mid-September 1956, I received the response. It was negative.

I called Montand immediately to transmit the bad news. He told me that he was not about to give up, and he wanted me to come to his house for lunch. He was not planning to say anything in public—yet.

A few days later I went to his residence, accompanied by an officer from the United States Information Service cultural office. I needed support. The residence was on the Isle de la Cité, a few blocks from Notre Dame cathedral, clearly a high-rent district.

Yves Montand was with his wife, the celebrated French actress Simone Signoret. I expected to receive a royal chewing out. But, not at all. Montand insisted that we find a solution. He considered the opportunity to do a Hollywood film with Marilyn Monroe the chance of a lifetime. He insisted that we find a solution. I told him that we needed to allow the dust to settle before we tried again. I promised to keep him informed.

A new opportunity arose in November 1956. It was not obvious at first. On November 4, the Soviet military undertook a massive invasion of the Hungarian capital, Budapest, along with several other cities. The communist government of Hungary had begun to slip away from Soviet control and influence, and it was starting to act independently.

About a week later, on a Sunday afternoon, I received a call from the Operations Center in the State Department. The department instructed me to travel immediately to Salzburg, Austria, to begin issuing visas to Hungarian refugees departing Hungary by the thousands to escape the Soviet invasion.

There were four of us processing the visa applications, including two Foreign Service officers who spoke fluent Hungarian: Les Tihany, who came from Tokyo, and Erny Nagy, who came from Frankfurt. A full-time interpreter accompanied me for the interviews.

In mid-December 1956 I returned to Paris, having issued several hundred refugee visas. Shortly after my return, I saw a newspaper headline that said the French Communist Party was organizing a demonstration in front of the Soviet Embassy to protest the invasion of Hungary. A light bulb flashed on. I immediately called Yves Montand and recommended that he join the protest and get himself photographed doing it. He followed my advice and was on all the front pages the next day.

I sent the articles and photos of Montand in the anti-Soviet demonstration to Washington. Within two days, Washington authorized his visa as a "defector from communism." Montand went to Hollywood and made the film *Let's Make Love*, co-starring Marilyn Monroe.

Yves Montand was not the only celebrity who had problems with the American visa law. One nightclub owner had been convicted under French law of collaboration with the Vichy regime during the German occupation of World War II. This made him ineligible for an American visa. He needed to travel to the U.S. regularly because he was in the process of replicating his French nightclub in Las Vegas. In those days obtaining a waiver for him was less difficult than for communists.

For the most part, the majority of refusal cases involved abortion. Until 1975, abortion was illegal in France, as it was in most of the American states. In 1955–1958, the headquarters of the North Atlantic Treaty Organization was located in the suburbs of Paris. With the presence of American military bases in various regions of France, a significant number of marriages between American military personnel and French women occurred. When these women applied for immigration visas to accompany their husbands to the United States, a small percentage had criminal records involving abortion. These convictions were the equivalent of felonies in the United States, making the spouses ineligible for immigration.

These family separations were true hardship cases. The only

solution was to persuade a member of Congress to introduce a special bill to allow the issuance of an immigration visa despite the felony conviction. After a while, these special bills became routine.

One of my most interesting experiences with American citizens visiting Paris involved a concert violinist who was giving several performances. One week when I was the duty officer, I took a call from the States from his wife. She told me that her husband had an extremely valuable Stradivarius violin and also that he was addicted to gambling. Fearing that he might end up gambling away his instrument, she asked if I could keep his violin in the Embassy between concerts. I am sure it was not allowed, but I said yes without checking. As a result, the violinist came to the Embassy to practice during the day, to the delight of both the American and French staff in the Consular Section.

As a young bachelor American diplomat, I found that Paris had a lot of opportunities in terms of social life. One of my fellow vice consuls in the Visa Section was a young lady from Washington, D.C., Marianne Cook. She shared a large apartment on the Boulevard de Courcelles with a young woman from Wyoming, Jane Evans, who worked in the embassy communications section. In late October 1955, they jointly decided to organize an American-style Thanksgiving dinner to show their French friends how we celebrated that particular holiday.

On Thanksgiving Day, the dinner began around 5 p.m. I was seated next to a young Frenchwoman named Suzanne. She had become friends with Marianne in a French-English conversation exchange program. During the dinner, I found that Suzanne's English was already quite fluent. During the main course, we were served artichokes. Growing up in New York City, I had never eaten this vegetable. I did not know what to do. Sensing my discomfort, Suzanne walked me through the process that ended with more being thrown away than eaten.

Suzanne and I started dating. When Foreign Service officers talk about their work, many people find it unusual or strange. But Suzanne understood right away, because her job was similar. She worked as middle management in charge of exports for a French pharmaceutical company, so all of her clients were in other countries.

When we became engaged, embassy security said that because Suzanne was not a U.S. citizen, a complete security investigation was required. That process took an entire year, so the wedding had to wait until April 1957.

We were married in the Reform Jewish synagogue on the rue Copernic on Friday afternoon, April 4. The entire consular department was closed at noon so that the staff could attend.

Under the rules at the time, my next assignment had to be in Washington so that my foreign citizen spouse could become naturalized. We left for Washington in September 1958 from the port of Cannes on the S.S. *America*. My three-year assignment in Paris as a visa officer had turned out to be a lot more interesting and eventful than I had imagined at the outset.

3

The World of Cultural Exchange

After our arrival in Washington in September 1958, we quickly found an apartment in North Arlington, Virginia, a few blocks from the Francis Scott Key Bridge. We signed a lease for a one-bedroom apartment in the Arlington Towers complex. Each of the complex's four buildings had a hundred apartments, garage parking, lounge areas, and twenty-four-hour reception service.

I was assigned to the State Department's Bureau of Educational and Cultural Affairs, which was responsible for administering all of the U.S. government's international cultural exchange programs. Best known was the Fulbright program, which brought foreign students and scholars to the United States for study and research at American colleges and universities and sent U.S. students and scholars abroad to study and teach at foreign institutions of higher learning.

Several other programs included invitations to foreign professionals in fields such as journalism, science, education, administration, and others to observe and exchange ideas with their American counterparts. American professionals were sent abroad to do the same in other countries.

The Bureau of Educational and Cultural Affairs, designated CU, was located in a State Department annex in the 1800 block of K Street NW, in the heart of the business district. Fortunately for me, a direct bus line from Arlington Towers to K street provided a fifteen-minute commute each way.

I was the first Foreign Service officer ever assigned to the CU Bureau. My job was to serve as the press and public information officer for the bureau and for all the bureau's international cultural, and educational exchange programs. I had one assistant press officer, who was a career civil servant, and one secretary, who was beginning a Foreign Service career.

We received a large amount of mail from Americans inquiring about opportunities for study or teaching abroad. We also heard from Americans interested in hosting foreign visitors. And we drafted public statements for senior officials who liked to talk about cultural exchange. One of our best clients was Senator William Fulbright of Arkansas, who liked to talk about the program that bore his name. On this subject, he preferred to have us write his speeches rather than have his own staff write them.

The Bureau of Educational and Cultural Exchange was an enjoyable place to work. The civil servants were all proud of the fact that they were implementing legislation designed to enhance cultural understanding among the peoples of many nations. What could be a higher calling in foreign affairs than that?

During one of my visits to the main State Department building, about five blocks away from our office, I ran into Madame Pekmazian, the head of the French language department of the Foreign Service Institute. She congratulated me for finally succeeding in reaching the passing grade in conversational French. I told her that I had married a French lady during my assignment in Paris. She asked to meet my wife, because she had a vacancy for a French instructor in her department. They had a meeting a short time later, and Suzanne was hired to join FSI's French language staff.

She was delighted to learn that the Foreign Service Institute language school was located on the lower floors of Arlington Towers. So, going to work every day consisted of riding the elevator. Suzanne became used to interacting with Foreign Service officers and their spouses, who spent up to six months with her for training. Some of them became good friends.

We also became friends with some of the other French instructors, who often joined us on weekends driving to southern Maryland's Point Lookout, at the mouth of the Potomac River, where we had picnic lunches. During 1958–1960, that region of Maryland included one of the few counties in the United States outside of Nevada that had legalized gambling. So we enjoyed playing the slot machines along the way to our destination.

About halfway through my assignment in CU, I needed to start thinking about my next step. In Paris, I had become friends with the embassy's labor attaché, who had many visa problems with French labor officials who wanted to visit their U.S. counterparts. I had helped him with those issues. My experience with him led me to consider becoming a labor attaché myself, in view of my New York working-class background.

I was accepted to the Foreign Service Institute academic year training course for labor attachés. The course consisted of internships with U.S. labor unions, interspersed with academic lectures at American University. During this nine-month period, I served six-week internships with the United Steelworkers in Providence, Rhode Island, and the Meat Cutters union in Chicago, Illinois. I also spent time with the International Affairs Bureau of the U.S. Department of Labor, which was responsible for U.S. membership in the International Labor Organization, and with the U.S. Department of Commerce, which enlightened me on the business view of labor relations.

During my time at the Labor Department, I learned that labor unions were playing an important political role in Africa, where approximately thirty-five British and French colonies were on the verge of becoming independent nations in 1960. I decided to investigate possible assignments in sub-Saharan Africa.

When I visited the newly organized Bureau of African Affairs in 1960, I learned that the International Confederation of Free Trade Unions (ICFTU), based in Brussels, Belgium, had decided to finance the establishment of the African Labor College, to be based in Kampala, Uganda. My contact in the Africa Bureau told me that there was a position open at the American Consulate General in Kampala for an administrative/consular officer. If I filled that position, I could cover the African Labor College at the same time.

I accepted the assignment to Kampala but could not depart immediately. First, I had to complete six months of Swahili language training at the Foreign Service Institute language school as one of two Foreign Service officers assigned to the course, the first in the history of the school. My colleague in training was John Anderegg, who was being assigned to Dar Es Salaam in Tanzania.

We spent six hours per day repeating Swahili dialogues with native speakers from Kenya, Tanzania, and the Congo. For the remaining two hours, we listened to Swahili tapes.

Swahili is an authentic African, or Bantu, language, with Arab language "borrowings." For example, the Arabic word for fish is "samak," the Swahili word is "samaki."

When the colonial powers began to carve up Africa at the beginning of the 1800s, they found that Swahili was the only African language that was written, using Arabic characters. In our training, we used Western script.

After six months, we took the examination in spoken Swahili. I managed to earn a passing grade of three, out of a possible five. The linguist in charge of the course said that I had succeeded because of my knowledge of the many different prefixes that are used by different nouns in the formulation of verbs in sentences. There is one noun, "rain," that enjoys a prefix not allowed to any other word. This demonstrates the importance of rain in East Africa.

Having completed all the training possible at that time, Suzanne and I left for Kampala in January 1962, right after New Year's. We left cold and rainy Washington and arrived two days later in hot and sunny Kampala on the Equator, at an altitude of one thousand meters. It was the beginning of eight uninterrupted years in four African countries.

4

GROWING A NEW EMBASSY IN KAMPALA, UGANDA

We stayed at the Imperial Hotel in downtown Kampala for a week while we awaited the cleaning and setting up of our assigned house on Kololo Hill, one of the upscale neighborhoods of the city.

During our first night, we were awakened at 5 a.m. by knocking at the door, followed by the entrance of a hotel staff person with a tray of tea and sandwiches. We expressed annoyance at being awakened so early.

The staffer said, "Sir, this is 'bed tea.' It comes automatically unless you cancel." We canceled.

In January 1962, the U.S. diplomatic presence in Uganda consisted of a consulate general. Since Uganda was still under British rule, we were not yet ready to establish an embassy. My job as administrative officer was, first, to make sure the consulate general had all the tools and personnel needed to carry out its mission. As the consular officer, I was in charge of supplying passport and protective services to all U.S. citizens in the consular district. I also took applications from persons not U.S. citizens or permanent U.S. residents for visas to travel to the United States.

Shortly after our arrival in Kampala, the State Department sent an instruction that we should prepare to change our status to an embassy as soon as Uganda became independent in October 1962. That included the assignment of ten additional officers and families from the U.S. Agency for International Development (USAID), and two additional cultural officers from the United States Information Agency (USIA). The State Department contingent was slated to increase by two persons, a United States ambassador and a full-time consular officer.

Thus, in addition to dealing with my regular duties, I had to start working on future requirements, which revolved around the search for staff housing and a new office to accommodate the new ambassador and his embassy staff.

The consul general had an elegant rental residence on Makerere Hill, on the north side of town. We decided to keep it for the future deputy chief of mission, and I was instructed to purchase it from the owner. I discovered that we were not eligible to purchase this property, because the land belonged to the kabaka of the Buganda ethnic nation. The kabaka was the equivalent of the king of England. Uganda was not designated as a British colony but as a British protectorate. The four separate monarchs in Uganda and their ethnic nations were under protective status and therefore enjoyed internal sovereignty. For that reason, we could sign a lease for the property, but we could not purchase it. We had to abide by the kabaka's rules.

The actual kabaka, at the time, was a young, very social Oxford-educated gentleman. He liked to be invited to receptions and dinners. We called him "King Freddy" when not addressing him as "Your Highness."

The search for an ambassadorial residence was difficult because all the other Western governments with diplomatic missions were doing the same thing. The competition was tough. I lost my first choice because the French government was able to complete the purchase very quickly, and they beat us to the deal.

The second residence, high on Kololo Hill, overlooking the city, was not as elegant but was the best we could do at the time. After Washington approved, I received a check for $75,000, a lot of money in 1962. We completed the purchase, and the State Department's Office of Foreign Buildings sent technical personnel to Kampala to prepare the residence according to our standards for health and security.

Two additional real estate challenges were for embassy office space and housing for the new staff. In this respect, we were lucky. The Ugandan government-in-waiting established a real estate development entity designed to make sure that housing would be available for the postindependence expanded international presence. We contracted with them for staff housing for twenty employees and a duplex embassy chancery in an office building reserved for foreign missions. We signed a lease for the top two floors, with an internal staircase that would create a single entity. We also signed a lease for staff housing, with a swimming pool for the secretaries and communication clerks and their families.

In July 1962, the new ambassador-designate, Olcott Deming, and his wife arrived to take charge of the mission, including preparations for our becoming an embassy. The work on the official residence was complete, so they were able to move in.

In the meantime, the Ugandan political system was gearing up to establish the nation's first independent postcolonial regime. Elections were held in August 1962 with the majority of votes going to the Uganda People's Congress, headed by Milton Obote, who was slated to be the nation's first president at independence.

In our own planning for independence ceremonies, we were informed that the U.S. delegation would be headed by the director of the United States Agency for International Development. This reflected the high priority overall U.S. policy toward Africa assigned to economic development.

We also believed that it would be advantageous for U.S.-Uganda relations if President Obote could be invited for an official visit with President Kennedy at an early date. We made this recommendation to the State Department as part of our overall package of post-independence proposals. The White House agreed to receive future President Obote for an official visit on October 22, 1962. Obote accepted with pleasure and made plans for travel.

The independence ceremony took place as scheduled a few minutes past midnight on October 9. The British representative who presided over the lowering of the British flag and the raising of the Ugandan flag was the Duchess of Kent.

Exactly one week later, the Cuban missile crisis erupted on October 16. The situation in Washington was quite tense. We were sure that President Obote's official visit would be postponed or even canceled. But to our surprise, the White House informed us that Obote should come ahead as planned. The visit took place, with Obote having lunch with President Kennedy, preceded by a meeting in the Cabinet room with advisers from both sides.

When President Obote returned to Kampala, Ambassador Deming organized a dinner in his honor with the embassy's entire American staff. During the dessert, the ambassador asked President Obote to give us his impressions of the visit to Washington. Obote heaped praise on President Kennedy, saying he could not believe how relaxed and unhurried Kennedy was in the midst of the missile crisis. Later, we learned that the White House had decided to go ahead with the visit because Kennedy wanted to project an image of business as usual. Having an official visitor from Africa during the crisis helped serve that purpose.

Between October 1962 and the end of the year, the embassy received its full complement of new American staff members, soon installed in the prearranged housing.

In June 1963, Suzanne and I welcomed the arrival of our first child, a boy whom we named Marc Andrew. His middle name was inspired by the British governor Sir Andrew Cohen, who left Uganda just after our arrival. Sir Andrew went on to become the head of the U.K. Office of Economic Development, the British equivalent of USAID.

The maternity facility at Mulago Hospital in Kampala was excellent, with separate kitchens for European, African, and Asian patients. The Asian population in Uganda was relatively large. Kampala's architecture was largely inspired by the architecture of India. Several British doctors at the hospital had come to Uganda to escape the socialization of medicine in Britain.

My predecessor at the Embassy had a pet dog, an Irish terrier named Piglet. He was unable to take Piglet with him to his next assignment in Nairobi, Kenya, because of the lengthy quarantine requirement. So, my wife and I agreed to adopt him. When our nanny took the baby for a daily walk in his carriage, Piglet made a point of walking in front of the carriage to make sure nobody approached too closely.

Piglet liked to bark, especially when African visitors came to the house. Our male housekeeper called Piglet "a white man's dog" because he barked only at Africans, not at Europeans. Once, when Piglet was barking excessively, I complained to our housekeeper. His response, in Swahili, was very characteristic. "Bwana, that is the dog's job. He is just doing his job."

I found time to pay visits to the newly established African Labor College of the International Confederation of Free Trade Unions. There, I met Tom Mboya, the Kenyan labor leader who played a major role in his country's independence movement. Within the limits of my small entertainment allowance, I was able to invite Ugandan labor leaders to lunch from time to time. They provided valuable insights into the complex relations between the political parties and Uganda's four kingdoms, as well as the large Rwandan Tutsi refugee community, which was destined to play a major role in the genocide of April 1994.

Early in our stay in Kampala, we made friends with Martin and Camille Aliker, a Ugandan-American couple and their family. Martin was a Ugandan dentist trained at Northwestern University in Chicago, with a practice in Kampala. Camille was an African American from New Rochelle, New York, who met her husband at the university. When we dined at their home, we were struck by their silverware, which displayed the initials "J.D."

Mrs. Aliker explained that she was a direct descendent of Jefferson Davis, the president of the Confederate States of America during the American Civil War. Her maternal ancestor had been a slave in Davis's home and inherited the silverware when Davis died. The silverware was passed down through several generations to Camille's mother.

With the arrival of a newly independent government, the embassy's relations with the political power system could not remain the same. A short time after independence, for example, the CIA station chief came to see me with a complaint: "I've lost my liaison." His easy relationship with the British intelligence service was not maintained with its Ugandan successor.

The administrative center of British East Africa was Nairobi, Kenya. Kampala was essentially a provincial town, while Nairobi was a major municipality. Because of this situation, international telephone communications shut down in Kampala at 8 p.m., essentially cutting us off from Washington for ten hours daily.

On November 22, 1963, as we dined at the CIA station chief's home, we knew something unusual had happened when the international telephone line suddenly opened at 10 p.m. We were informed then that President Kennedy had been assassinated.

The death of an American president requires a number of actions by all American embassies around the world. We took the first action the next morning when we opened a condolence book. Very early, there was a long line of Ugandans waiting to enter the Embassy to sign the book. We also sent the embassy's condolences to the Kennedy family in Washington. We wrote a formal diplomatic note to the foreign minister officially informing him of the event and that Vice President Lyndon Johnson had been sworn in as president. We also reassured the Ugandan government that we anticipated no change in the state of our relations.

Overall, we were off to a good start in our diplomatic relations with the new nation of Uganda. I was happy to have played a role in the preparations. With our one-year-old baby son in his basket, we took leave of Uganda in January 1964 to transfer to the British colony of Southern Rhodesia. I was designated to be the regional labor attaché, covering Southern Rhodesia, Northern Rhodesia, and Malawi, all still British colonies when we arrived.

5

Fighting White Supremacy in Salisbury, Southern Rhodesia

Suzanne and I arrived in what was then Salisbury, Southern Rhodesia, in January 1964. After livng in the relatively small city of
Kampala, Uganda, for two years, we found Salisbury to be a major
city, with a broad central boulevard, wide adjoining avenues, and
high-rise office buildings of up to twenty-five stories. It was compa-
rable to a midsized American town of around 100,000 people.

To an American diplomat, Southern Rhodesia's significance
was its membership in what was known as "white minority–ruled
southern Africa." The other countries in this category at the time
were South Africa, Angola, Mozambique, and Southwest Africa
(now Namibia). Southwest Africa was a UN Trust Territory, placed
under South African jurisdiction as a mandate shortly after the First
World War. South Africa administered the territory essentially as
an integrated part of itself, including its strict racial segregation
system of *apartheid.*

Like South Africa, Southern Rhodesia practiced racial segregation, but of a less severe kind. Certain hotels and restaurants were
designated as multiracial, but the majority were segregated. In post
offices and banks, there were separate lines for whites and non-
whites.

The independent African countries to the north of Southern
Rhodesia had as their highest political priority the liberation of
their African brethren living under white minority rule. In Southern Rhodesia African political movements lived within the law, but
their leadership was often placed in detention when their public
statements were deemed extreme. Black labor unions were legal,
with their leadership affiliated with the political movements. The

job that I was assigned to fill involved contacts with the labor unions as a window into the political undercurrents within the black majority community.

The American consulate general in Salisbury did everything possible to demonstrate disapproval of racial segregation. For that reason, my family and I were placed in the city's only multiracial hotel, the Jameson, while we looked for a rental house in the nearby suburbs. We were quite comfortable in the hotel, with the equivalent of a two-bedroom apartment.

The consulate general was located on the top two floors of the Central Bank building. with the lower floor devoted to consular affairs and administration. The consul general and the political and economic sections were on the upper floor. We were quite comfortable in this space, with lots of room to accommodate visitors.

As the regional labor officer covering Southern Rhodesia, Northern Rhodesia, and Nyasaland, I had my own quite ample travel budget. As of January 1964, all three territories were still British colonies. In October of that year, Britain granted Northern Rhodesia and Nyasaland their independence, and they changed their names to Zambia and Malawi respectively. It was not until 1980 that Southern Rhodesia, then known only as Rhodesia, gained its independence, under black majority rule, with the new name Zimbabwe.

We found a three-bedroom house in the upscale Highlands suburb, located five miles from Salisbury, with ample parking in the neighborhood. The plot of land was large, with lots of room for outdoor events. We also found a nanny for our infant son Marc. The daily commute to the office took about twenty minutes one way.

There were two labor union federations, one black and one white. The white labor union members worked mainly on the railroads and in the industries located in the southwestern city of Bulawayo. While Salisbury was the capital, with government bureaucracy, political party headquarters, financial institutions, and major business enterprises, Bulawayo was the center for manufacturing and processing, where the whites dominated. The black union members dominated in all enterprises that were not in Bulawayo. For example, they were the main union on the railroad operating out of Salisbury. They dominated all businesses in Salisbury, including retail, public transport, hotels, and restaurants.

Overall, the Rhodesian economy was based mainly on commercial agriculture. The commercial farmers, who were all members of the white minority, produced maize, fruits, vegetables, and above all Virginia tobacco. Rhodesia was the second largest global exporter of Virginia tobacco after the United States. It was interesting to see American tobacco auctioneers coming to Rhodesia in November every year to sell that year's Rhodesian crop. Much of it went to Asia. Also of significance were the citrus groves in the southeast in a low-lying area called the *lowveld*. In contrast to the rest of Rhodesia, which was on a high plateau extending from South Africa, the *lowveld* was closer to sea level, with a subtropical climate equivalent to Florida.

In addition to a strong agricultural sector, Rhodesia's chrome had a strong worldwide market. The United States was a major chrome importer.

In the political realm, Southern Rhodesia was a self-governing British colony, with a governor general appointed by London from the white Rhodesian community. When we arrived in January 1964, the moderate, centrist United Party controlled the white Rhodesian government, and the three colonies were loosely grouped together as the Central African Federation. The white Rhodesian prime minister was Sir Roy Welensky. As far as we could tell, the only evidence of the federation was the international Central African Airlines.

There was tension in the air in early 1964 because the British government had announced that Northern Rhodesia and Nyasaland would become independent nations in October 1964. When the white minority regime in Southern Rhodesia asked, "What about us?" the British replied that independence would not be possible until the political system transitioned from white minority rule to black majority rule. This caused a major upheaval in white minority politics.

In mid-1964, the white Rhodesian citizens held an election. A far rightwing party, the Rhodesian Front, replaced the moderate United Party in power. It was an expression of resentment against the British for its refusal to acknowledge that the white Rhodesians were totally ready for independence. The winning party leader was Ian Smith, a farmer and World War II veteran RAF pilot. Combat injuries had resulted in permanent paralysis of half his face. And he was clearly ready to take a hard line against British rule.

My contacts with the labor union leadership were easy. Both the leaders and many of the workers were happy to talk to a representative of the United States government. I had the same warm welcome from both black and white labor unions. Unsurprisingly, the labor union people were consistently more interested in talking about politics than collective bargaining or working conditions.

Toward the end of 1964, Suzanne and I decided to host a cocktail reception for the labor leadership, both white and black. In addition to the labor leaders, we invited the white minister of labor. Judging from the animated discussions, the party was successful. As he was leaving, the minister thanked me for helping him meet with black labor leaders for the first time.

Increasing levels of political tension within Southern Rhodesia marked the first half of 1965. Neighboring Northern Rhodesia and Nyasaland had become independent Zambia and Malawi. The UK high commissioner told us about his fear that the white Rhodesians would declare their independence, which would be illegal under both British and international law and would trigger a major crisis. In March 1965, British prime minister Harold Wilson came to Salisbury to take the temperature. He spent a full three days in Salisbury, an unprecedented event for a UK head of government.

At one point during the prime minister's visit, our informant at the British High Commission told us, Wilson grabbed Rhodesian PM Ian Smith by the lapels and screamed, "Are you going to declare independence or not?" A few months after his departure, Harold Wilson, received an answer to his question. On November 11, 1965, the Government of Southern Rhodesia announced that henceforth it would consider Rhodesia an independent nation. It had been self-governing since 1923. For public consumption, the event was shortened to UDI, Unilateral Declaration of Independence.

The British were livid but not surprised. They immediately declared UDI to be illegal. They sent their navy to blockade the Mozambique port of Beira that controlled the entry of the pipeline that supplied crude oil to the Rhodesian refinery in the city of Umtali on the Rhodesian-Mozambique border, thereby cutting off Rhodesia's main source of fuel. International trade could not be stopped, however, because Rhodesia had a land border with South Africa that could not be blocked.

The U.S. reaction to UDI. was equally severe. Sanctions were applied that prohibited trade with Rhodesia. Washington also reduced the size of the American consulate general, abolishing the position of consul general and transferring almost all American personnel elsewhere. A consul headed the small staff that remained.

Since I covered both Zambia and Malawi as the regional labor attaché, I was transferred to the American Embassy in Lusaka, Zambia, as the economic/ commercial officer. About two weeks after UDI, we arranged to have our household furniture crated and sent to South Africa for storage. We packed our personal effects and, with our two-year-old son, set out for Lusaka by road in our small Fiat sedan.

We knew we would miss Rhodesia because of the friendly people of all races, and because of the great weather on the high plateau and the beautiful vistas. The availability of large sacks of locally grown oranges for the equivalent of three American dollars ranked high on our list of regrets.

6

THE END OF COLONIALISM IN
LUSAKA, ZAMBIA

We arrived in Lusaka, Zambia, after a six-hour road trip from Salisbury. The final segment of the drive included a bridge crossing of the mighty Zambezi River, which originates at the famous Victoria Falls.

We soon found that Zambia was feeling pain because of the sanctions that the British had imposed on Rhodesia. Most important, Zambia's only source of petroleum products came from the Rhodesian refinery in Umtali that had been closed by the British blockade of Beira. The first information the U.S. embassy in Lusaka provided was that I would be limited to the purchase of no more than four gallons of gasoline per month for my automobile. For that reason, the embassy arranged for its American employees to be picked up every morning by bus.

Lusaka was very much like Salisbury, with a broad central avenue and wide side streets but on a much smaller scale. The building heights were much lower. Most important was the total absence of racial segregation.

The first American ambassador accredited to the new Republic of Zambia was Robert C. Good, a Johnson administration political appointee from Denver, Colorado. Dr. Good was a professor of African studies at the University of Denver, one of the most important graduate schools of international relations in the United States. He had been the state chairman of the 1960 Kennedy-Johnson presidential campaign in Colorado.

We did not have to house-hunt in Lusaka as we moved directly into the house the departing economic commercial officer, Larry Williamson, and family had vacated. Located about a ten-minute drive from downtown Lusaka, the house was in the upscale suburb of Woodlands, where virtually all of the residents were expatriates from Europe, mainly Britain. As in Rhodesia, Zambia's residents of European origin had been there for several generations. They were well organized, with religious houses of worship and various types of active business, including agriculture. Unlike in Rhodesia, the Zambian whites were psychologically ready for black majority rule and appeared quite comfortable with the idea.

Ambassador Good was full of enthusiasm for Zambia and fervently opposed to the *apartheid* regime in South Africa. He believed that a successful Zambia would demonstrate to the white people of South Africa that they had nothing to fear from black majority rule. His assignment to me, therefore, as the economic-commercial officer, was to promote U.S. private investments.

Our first order of business was to help Zambia overcome the hardships flowing from the blockade of the Umtali oil refinery in Rhodesia. Refined oil products were coming in by road from neighboring Zaire to the north. But the quantity was insufficient for road traffic to return to normal in Zambia. So, we requested funding to bring in oil products by air from Zaire. To our great surprise, the money was allocated, and we began to fill our gas tanks again.

Then there was the issue of Zambia's copper exports. At that time, Zambia was the second biggest exporter of copper in the world after Chile. Out of concern that potential political instability in southern Africa could seriously disrupt world copper markets, the Chilean government maintained an embassy in Lusaka. Zambian copper was exported by rail via Southern Rhodesia to the port of Lourenço Marques in Portuguese-controlled Mozambique. The Zambians were fearful that their most important source of revenue could be held for ransom by the white minority Rhodesian regime. Ambassador Good thus insisted on our finding a safe alternate export route.

We looked at several alternatives. These included the railway north through Katanga in Zaire, the railway south through Botswana to the South African port of Cape Town, and northeast through Tanzania to the port of Dar Es Salaam. The Zaire route was rejected because the cargo would have to be transferred to a river barge halfway through and then back again to rail on the final leg. The route through Botswana to Cape Town was efficient, but the Zambians did not want to be dependent on the white South Africans.

That left the route to the northeast, through Tanzania, as the only viable alternative. The trouble with that option was that there was neither a road nor a rail connection. Everything would have to start from zero. That did not faze Ambassador Good, who directed us to study the possibilities of financing either a road or a rail connection.

We concluded that a railroad would be the most efficient and secure way of exporting Zambian copper through Tanzania and presented our proposal to USAID in Washington. Because of overall budgetary constraints, they decided instead to help finance a road, because it would be much less expensive than a railroad. To our great surprise, USAID agreed to finance the road.

Meanwhile, I was pursuing my mandate to promote U.S. private investments in Zambia. I started by doing an inventory of all U.S.-owned private companies. I found ten such companies, none of which had American personnel. The most significant was a copper mining company, Roan Selection Trust (RST), which was owned by St. Joe Minerals of St. Louis. Except for RST, all of the U.S. companies in Zambia reported to higher authority in Johannesburg, South Africa. Because of the political instability caused by the Rhodesian situation, no new American companies showed interest in establishing enterprises in Zambia at that time.

During June 1966, Foreign Service inspectors arrived at the Embassy on a routine visit, which happens in every American Embassy in the world about every four or five years. The inspectors interview the American employees regarding their careers and their experience at the embassy. And they conduct an audit of the embassy's finances.

During the inspectors' interview with me, they noted that my career specialization was in the field of labor. In Zambia, labor reporting was only a minor element in my work as an economic officer. They pointed out that there was a vacancy for a fulltime labor attaché in the U.S. embassy in Kinshasa, in neighboring Zaire. They recommended that I transfer there and proceeded to arrange it.

In September 1966, my family and I arrived in Kinshasa, Zaire, via Pan American Airways from Johannesburg, South Africa, to find the embassy in Kinshasa in a state of turmoil.

7

Coping with Chaos in Kinshasa, Zaire (Congo)

When we arrived at the Kinshasa airport at 3 p.m. on September 15, 1966, we were informed that we were invited to a reception at the ambassador's residence at 6 p.m. that same evening. It was a farewell party for departing ambassador Mac Godley. His leaving was not at all routine—President Mobutu had declared him *persona non grata.* Mobutu had become fed up with the ambassador's constant harping about corruption and mismanagement. The embassy staff had already arranged for a babysitter for our three-year-old son Marc.

Ambassador Godley's falling out with President Mobutu should not have been a surprise in view of the special relationship between the United States and the former Belgian Congo since the country's independence on June 30, 1960. The entire independence process had been chaotic at best, and the United States had been constantly dealing with crises. An activist, Mac Godley felt free to express his views on Zaire's internal affairs.

After eighteen months of such treatment, President Mobutu no longer stood in awe of the United States and decided that Godley was no longer welcome. After Godley departed, and pending the assignment of a new ambassador, Deputy Chief of Mission Robert Blake became chargé d'affaires, the acting head of the embassy.

After taking the family and our luggage to our embassy house, I got to work immediately in the Political Section as the labor attaché. The chief of the political section, Harvey Nelson, informed me that within a few months he would be rotating to a new job as the U.S. ambassador in Swaziland and that the State Department director for Central African affairs, Dean Brown, would be coming to Kinshasa for a week's visit. As I began to arrange meetings with Zaire's large crop of labor union leaders, I experienced a few things that had nothing to do with my labor responsibilities.

One day, the embassy receptionist asked me to see a lady who was insisting that we find a way to get her husband out of President Mobutu's prison on an island in the Atlantic Ocean. His name was Cléophas Kamitatu, from the province of Bandundu, and he was apparently there for political reasons. I agreed to receive Mrs. Kamitatu as a courtesy. After her long explanation of what had happened, I said that the embassy could not become involved in an internal political situation and that I could not be of assistance.

Mrs. Kamitatu persisted and would not take no for an answer. In order to persuade her to leave, I relented and said we would see what we could do. As fate would have it, Kamitatu was released one week later. The embassy had nothing to do with his release, but Mrs. Kamitatu started spreading the word that the American diplomat Herman Cohen was responsible. I had become an instant hero in Kinshasa's political community. That incident constituted the beginning of my long-lasting relationship with the politics of Zaire, later renamed the Democratic Republic of the Congo.

Shortly after Robert Blake took over as chargé d'affaires, I received a visit from the CIA station chief, Larry Devlin, who said he met regularly with President Mobutu. From time to time, Mobutu would call and ask him to come by the Presidency. Devlin's problem was that Robert Blake had issued an order that only the chief of mission would be authorized to meet with President Mobutu. In other words, Devlin was no longer allowed to visit his friend Mobutu. Devlin explained that the order effectively made his situation impossible. If he could no longer meet with Mobutu, he could not remain with the embassy. He would have to request a transfer.

At Devlin's behest I intervened with Blake, who was quite frank. In his view, the head of state should not have several channels of contact with the United States. If Mobutu were unhappy with what he heard from the U.S. ambassador, he could turn to the CIA station chief in hopes that he would hear a different point of view. Blake considered a situation of that kind unacceptable. I agreed with him and so informed Devlin, who immediately requested a transfer.

Devlin's deputy, Frank Jeton, became acting station chief. He, too, had a close relationship with Mobutu, but he was able to live with the directive that he should stop seeing the president privately.

In November 1966, we had a visit from Central African Affairs Director Dean Brown. Since Zaire was the biggest and most important country in his portfolio, he stayed with us an entire week. At the end of his stay, he said he wanted me to replace Harvey Nelson, the outgoing head of the embassy political section. Brown had seen me working with labor union leaders and considered me qualified to head the section. Needless to say, I was quite happy with the "battlefield promotion."

In February 1967, Robert Blake went on a ski vacation for one month, and I became acting chargé. Shortly after Blake's departure, Mobutu issued a decree nationalizing the copper mines owned by the Belgian company Union Minière du Haut Katanga (UMHK). The revenue from this company and the royalties it paid to the regime were the government's main source of wealth. Under international law, the Zaire government had the right to nationalize private property, but the payment of compensation was required. What made Mobutu's decision a crisis, was his statement that the Government of Zaire would not pay compensation.

The UMHK immediately withdrew all of its expatriate employees. Since there were no Zairian employees in managerial positions, all production stopped, which meant that most financial flows to the government would stop as well. Nevertheless, the nationalization was popular with the people, as shown by pro-Mobutu demonstrations in the streets of Kinshasa. Students from the Louvanium University came down from their mountain to demonstrate as well. The big challenge was to find a way to enable Mobutu to pay compensation without losing prestige among the population. As acting chief of mission, I asked the embassy Economic Section to brainstorm the problem. They came up with a creative proposal. Since the mine could not continue operating without the expatriate managers, Mobutu should contract with another Belgian company to run the mine. The basic cost of the contract would be increased 20 percent so as to generate surplus funds with which to reimburse UMHK for the nationalization without public knowledge. Since the compensation would be hidden, Mobutu would not suffer a political backlash.

A few days later, the president of the World Bank, Robert Mc-
Namara, came to Kinshasa to try to help solve the problem. His
first request was to talk to the American embassy chief of mission. I
went to see him in his hotel room and presented him with our proposed solution. I also suggested that he be the one to recommend it
to Mobutu. He agreed.

McNamara went to the southeastern city of Lubumbashi, in
the heart of the copper mining region, to meet with Mobutu, who
agreed to the proposal. With our assistance, Mobutu contracted
with the Belgian company Société Générale des Minerais, which
took over management of the mines. Thus, for the time being the
problem was solved. Looking to the future, Mobutu arranged to
send several students to the Colorado School of Mines to obtain
degrees in mining engineering.

In April 1967, we received a message signed by President Lyndon Johnson informing us that former vice president Richard Nixon would be traveling in Africa and that one of his stops would be
Kinshasa. Such a direct communication to a U.S. embassy from the
president is most unusual. Johnson wanted us to give Nixon the
highest VIP treatment.

Chargé Robert Blake arranged some high-level meetings for
Nixon, including a lunch with President Mobutu. Blake asked Nixon, as a special request, if he would have lunch with the embassy's American staff, who would be thrilled to meet the former vice
president. The lunch took place at Blake's residence and was quite
congenial. At the end, both Blake and Nixon made remarks. Nixon
pointed out that he and Blake came from the same town, Whittier,
California. He had followed Blake's career and expected him to go
on to greater glories.

After Nixon's departure, I told Blake that if Nixon ever became
president he would be in an excellent position. Blake responded, in
his nonchalant way, that he was also in a good situation with the
Democrats, because his wife, Sylvia, was a member of the powerful
Whitehouse family of Rhode Island.

In March 1967, we took a few weeks off to go to Paris, where our
second child was born, a boy named Alain.

In April 1967, a new ambassador, Robert McBride, arrived in
Kinshasa to represent the United States. He had just been the dep-

uty chief of mission of the American Embassy in Paris, one of the largest American diplomatic missions in the world. A week after McBride's arrival, Robert Blake departed to become the U.S. ambassador to the Republic of Mali. To replace Blake as DCM, McBride arranged to bring Ralph McGuire, who had been with him in Paris as the political-military officer.

Shortly after McBride's arrival, so-called Marxist insurgents invaded eastern Zaire. They operated in the hills opposite Tanzania, attacking villages and government installations. Mobutu's military were doing a fairly good job of containing the insurgents but suffered from a major logistics problem. They were one thousand miles away from their supply sources, and transportation was weak.

On the advice of his country team, Ambassador McBride requested U.S. military transport aircraft be deployed to Kinshasa to be used for supply trips to the troops in the east. Because of the domestic political problems caused by the Vietnam War, the issue had to be sent to President Johnson for decision. Johnson approved the deployment of two C-130 transport aircraft for a period of three months.

After the aircraft arrived, the embassy set up a system to organize daily flights, coordinated by the defense attaché and me, in my role as political counselor. The operation went on for three months, during which time the insurgents became tired and withdrew. Only about a dozen times did we refuse specific requests from the Zaire military, lest we bring our personnel too close to the fighting.

In October 1967, we had a visit from Joseph Palmer, the assistant secretary of state for Africa, who was making a five-nation tour of Africa. Ambassador McBride happened to be away on consultations in Washington, so Secretary Palmer stayed at DCM McGuire's residence. The visit was uneventful, with Palmer seeing Mobutu and all the other senior politicians.

Ambassador McBride returned in early November. Later that month, he received a personal letter from Secretary Palmer recommending a transfer for DCM McGuire. Palmer believed that the DCM was not happy in Africa and that he should go to another region of the world. McBride complied and arranged for the transfer.

Afterward, McBride talked to me about the future. He told me that he would not be requesting the assignment of a new DCM. During his own consultations in the State Department, he arranged to be selected as ambassador to Mexico. In view of his forthcoming departure, he asked me to serve as acting DCM until a new ambassador and DCM could arrive.

McBride's departure for Mexico took place in June 1968, and I became the acting chief of mission, the chargé d'affaires *ad interim*. Because McBride's departure was not in accordance with the normal three-year tour of duty, a replacement ambassador was not waiting in the wings. For that reason, I remained in charge of the embassy for a full year before a new ambassador could be assigned.

My year as head of mission was uneventful, with not a single crisis. I had many opportunities to meet with President Mobutu when taking high-ranking visitors to meet him, including Vice President Hubert Humphrey. I remember one call on Mobutu in particular, in late 1968, for a breakfast meeting at which Mobutu served us Scotch whiskey. He had his ear glued to a radio listening to the results of the French presidential election and was extremely happy to announce to us that Pompidou was the winner.

In June 1969, a new American ambassador was finally assigned to Kinshasa. He was Sheldon Vance, who was coming from the embassy in Brussels, where he had been the second in command. We advised him in advance that he would need to wear a morning coat and striped pants for the presentation of credentials to President Mobutu. After he arrived, I learned that he had forgotten to bring the correct outfit. This resulted in my final crisis in Kinshasa before my own departure.

Ambassador Vance was six feet six inches tall. Where were we going to find a morning outfit of that size? Someone suggested that we ask the Danish ambassador, who was about the same height. It turned out that he still had his morning coat and was willing to lend it to Ambassador Vance. Unfortunately, despite the similar height, many alterations had to be made, such that the Danish ambassador could no longer use it. Nevertheless, he was most gracious about having given assistance to a NATO ally.

We departed Kinshasa shortly thereafter for Paris to spend a few days with Suzanne's family before going to Washington for a new assignment in the State Department. As we arrived in our hotel, we were able to watch the first moon landing, which we later celebrated over a champagne dinner with Suzanne's family. It was a wonderful way to finish eight straight years of duty in Africa.

When I returned to Washington for an assignment in the State Department's Bureau of African Affairs, I was informed that anyone who serves as chargé d'affaires for nine months or longer receives credit for having officially been chief of mission. Accordingly, my chances for promotion had been greatly enhanced.

8

MAKING POLICY IN WASHINGTON

After serving eight years at four American missions in Africa, I had no alternative but to serve a tour of duty in the State Department in Washington. After a few weeks of "home leave" vacation during the summer of 1969, I reported for duty in the State Department's Bureau of African Affairs in September 1969.

During our vacation, we purchased our first home in the Georgetown neighborhood of Washington, about fifteen minutes' drive from the State Department. We enrolled our six-year-old son Marc in the first grade at the Maret School. Our two-year-old second son, Alain, helped his mom set up our new house.

My State Department assignment was to the Office of Central African Affairs, AF/C. The African countries covered by the office included all the French speaking nations of Central Africa plus Madagascar and Mauritius. The Republic of Zaire generated the most work for the office. It was normal that I would be assigned to AF/C following my three years in Zaire.

My job in AF/C was deputy director and officer in charge of Zaire, Rwanda, and Burundi, the three former Belgian colonies.

The director of AF/C, and my immediate boss, was John McKesson, a veteran senior Foreign Service officer.

John was born into the McKesson pharmaceutical family. His father had decided not to join the company, opting instead to study painting in Paris. John grew up in Paris, doing all his primary and secondary schooling in French language schools. Consequently, he was totally bilingual.

John did his postsecondary studies at Columbia University in New York. He performed his required military service in the U.S.

Navy and joined the U.S. Foreign Service immediately thereafter. During an assignment to Iceland, he married an Icelandic woman, with whom he had a son.

During my first year in AF/C, 1969–1970, John encouraged me to travel to our countries to get acquainted, putting me on travel status for as much as three weeks at a time. I also had two special assignments that first year in AF/C. We received "private" visits from two senior African leaders: the president of Cameroon and the foreign minister of Madagascar. Both wanted to tour the United States, and I was assigned to escort them and act as their French-English interpreter. These visits were totally "unofficial."

Since Cameroon is an oil-producing country, the visit of President Ahmadou Ahidjo was of interest to American oil companies. They volunteered to supply their executive aircraft and crews to transport Ahidjo and his entourage to various U.S. destinations. As Ahidjo did not like to spend time in conversation, there was not much talking on the airplanes. He did, however, like to talk to American government and business leaders whom he met. He received lavish hospitality at every stop.

In New Orleans, Ahidjo was invited to visit an offshore oil platform in the Gulf of Mexico operated by the Chevron Corporation. Among the workers on the platform were a number of "Cajuns" who spoke French. In anticipation of Ahidjo's visit, Chevron mobilized a group of Cajuns to greet him in French.

Ahidjo flew to the offshore platform via helicopter from Lake Pontchartrain north of New Orleans. On the platform he was surrounded by Cajuns, who engaged him in conversation. Later that evening, during dinner, he told me that he could not understand a word they said.

During a visit to Houston, Texas, the mayor invited Ahidjo to dinner in the owner's box at the football stadium, while a college football game was in progress. At the end of the dinner, Ahidjo thanked the mayor for the dinner and conversation. When the mayor asked him his impression of the football game, Ahidjo said, "I find it very cruel."

The visit of Foreign Minister Didier Ratsiraka of Madagascar was markedly different. Ratsiraka was an angry man with a chip on his shoulder. He did not belong to the elite Merina ethnic group, the descendants of Polynesian immigrants from the south Pacific who lived on the high plateau and controlled political power. Instead, he was from the coastal peoples, who were mixed Asian and African.

The main U.S. interest in Madagascar lay in an Air Force tracking station that was important for watching our many satellites in space. Driven by his anti-imperialist nonaligned sentiments, Ratsiraka was determined to close it down.

Our uneventful and relaxed trip around the United States was entirely by commercial airlines. The foreign minister enjoyed his different experiences. During our conversations, he told me that he was determined to take power in Madagascar.

At the end of the trip, Ratsiraka had a full day and evening in Washington. The day before, he requested that I take him to a "detective store." I asked him what he was looking for specifically. He said that he was sure that wherever he traveled, "the French" were spying on him. He wanted one or more devices that would prevent anyone from listening to his conversations. I found the store for him but did not join him for the shopping.

After Ratsiraka returned to Madagascar, he gave notice that we would have to close the satellite tracking station at the end of the lease period. When I consulted the U.S. Air Force about the issue, they said they were moving away from ground stations and would be tracking satellites from other satellites. So, we did not put up any resistance.

After I had been in AF/C for a full year, and after I had visited every one of the countries we covered, John McKesson was named ambassador to the Republic of Gabon. He recommended that I be named his replacement as director. Assistant Secretary of State for Africa David Newsom agreed, and I moved into the director's chair.

Since Gabon was one of the countries that we covered in AF/C, I was in regular touch with Ambassador McKesson. After two months, I asked if he felt comfortable. He said that he was having a problem with language. Since he had grown up in France and gone to French schools, he spoke French like a Frenchman. This caused suspicion among the Gabonese, who were used to the American ambassador speaking French with an American accent. Some of his Gabonese contacts were worried that the French government had managed to slip one of their people into the American embassy.

The largest country in our central African portfolio was Zaire (which in 1996 became the Democratic Republic of the Congo). In 1972, the American ambassador to the Vatican received a request for help. In Zaire, President Mobutu and Cardinal Malula, the archbishop of Kinshasa, were not on good terms. Even worse, they hated each other. Mobutu was furious about some criticism that Malula was uttering during Sunday sermons, being especially critical of high-level governmental corruption. Mobutu found this unacceptable.

I decided to go to Kinshasa, with a stopover in Rome, to see if the U.S. government might be helpful. When I entered the offices of the Vatican Foreign Ministry, I was blown away by the many art masterpieces by such painters as Raphael, Van Gogh, and Pissarro. In my first meeting with the Foreign Ministry officials, I apologized for not speaking Italian. The response was reassuring. "This is the Foreign Ministry. We speak French here."

My proposal for an initial solution to the problem of Cardinal Malula was for the Vatican to recall him to Rome for a year-long sabbatical. My Vatican colleagues agreed, but they feared that Mobutu would not let him return. They encouraged me to go to Kinshasa to reason with Mobutu.

During my three-year tour in the U.S. Embassy in Kinshasa, I had developed a good relationship with Mobutu. So, I felt relaxed about talking to him on a sensitive issue.

Mobutu greeted me warmly, but he became animated and emotional when the conversation turned to the Malula problem. "Where does he come off accusing me of corruption? I have a list of all of his mistresses. I feel that he is the corrupt person."

After I listened to Mobutu destroy Malula's character and reputation, I suggested we allow the situation to cool down. I told Mobutu that the Vatican was willing to summon Malula to Rome for a year-long sabbatical, provided they had Mobutu's guarantee that the cardinal would be allowed to return. Mobutu was happy to be rid of the "nasty" cardinal, if only for a year. He therefore was willing to have me transmit his guarantee that Malula would be allowed to return.

On my way back to Washington, I stopped in Rome to report on my meeting with Mobutu that provided a positive outcome for

Cardinal Malula. The Foreign Ministry officials expressed their gratitude and gave me a private tour of the Vatican Museum, as well as St. Peter's Basilica.

I asked them if they were aware that President Houphouët-Boigny of Côte d'Ivoire had spent a tremendous amount of money to build a full-scale replica of St. Peter's in central Côte d'Ivoire near the town of Yammasoukro. The officials complained unhappily that the president requested that the pope come to the jungle to dedicate the African version of his basilica. The pope was not enthusiastic, because so much money went to the basilica that should have been used instead to alleviate poverty.

Back in Kinshasa, tensions were greatly reduced, at least for a year.

In Madagascar, Foreign Minister Ratsiraka was doing everything he could to hurt U.S.-Malagasy relations. He called in the U.S. ambassador, Anthony Marshall, and told him that the U.S. Air Force satellite-tracking station had to be closed within one year. Marshall, a Johnson administration political appointee, argued that the order constituted a violation of the bilateral agreement. Marshall made considerable noise to the point that he was ordered to leave the county. In short, U.S-Malagasy relations had reached rock bottom.

Shortly thereafter, the Malagasy hierarchy had second thoughts. The president of the country, Gabriel Ramanantsoa, decided to make an informal visit to Washington. To show that we had no hard feelings, we organized a high-level reception in his honor. When he entered the room, he spotted my wife Suzanne, and they fell into a hug. Before she married me and joined me in the U.S. Foreign Service, Suzanne managed the export department of a French pharmaceutical company. Before entering politics, President Ramanantsoa was a pharmacist who imported drugs from Suzanne's company. They were old friends.

We informed Ramanantsoa that our need for the tracking station was phasing out and we would be closing it soon. He accepted this, and relations warmed up after we sent a new ambassador.

***

During my five years as director of Central African Affairs, my biggest lapse of judgment involved the Republic of Cameroon. I continue to regret it to this day.

Until the end of World War One, Germany had been a colonial power in Africa, over Tanganyika, Rwanda, Burundi, Togo, Southwest Africa, and Cameroon. As the defeated power, Germany lost all its African colonies, which all became mandates of the League of Nations, and later of the United Nations.

Under the United Nations, Cameroon was administered as two separate regions. The majority French-speaking region was administered by France. The minority English-speaking region was administered as part of Nigeria by the United Kingdom.

In 1960, France granted independence to Cameroon, and Britain granted independence to Nigeria. That left the English-speaking former German colony. The British decided to offer the people of anglophone Cameroon a choice via referendum. Join Nigeria or join Cameroon. Independence was not an option.

The result of the referendum was to join Cameroon. Because of the language difference, the British decided to establish a federal arrangement within which the English-speaking community would have a large degree of autonomy. They would have their own parliament, and a prime minister who would also be the vice president of all of Cameroon.

Between 1960 and 1972, this federal arrangement worked well. In 1972, unfortunately, the president of Federal Cameroon, Ahmadou Ahidjo, decided that he wanted to have a one-party state similar to the majority of African countries. Why should Cameroon be different? He held a referendum to decide between maintaining or abolishing the federation. With three quarters of the voters being francophones, the federation was abolished by a large majority. President Ahidjo was then free to establish a single-party state in line with the majority of the other African governments.

There was not much change for the average Cameroonian citizen after the referendum. Over time, however, the English speakers felt the weight of discrimination, both economically and culturally. It took over thirty years, but the situation ultimately became so bad for the anglophones that violence broke out, with full-scale civil war developing in the year 2018.

My mistake and regret were that we did not object to the referendum and the breakup of the federation. After all, the English speakers had voted to join a federal system in their UN-sponsored referendum of 1960. Ahidjo's referendum of 1972 was essentially a violation of the 1960 decision made under UN auspices. As of mid-2022, the Cameroon civil war was showing no signs of ending.

Toward the end of 1974, it was time for me to start thinking about going abroad again. In those days, five years was the maximum for a Washington assignment. I went to see my personnel counselor to look at the available options. I asked, "Where in Africa do you intend to assign me?" His response came as a big surprise. "For you, going back to Africa is strictly forbidden. Secretary of State Kissinger has issued an order."

I asked why Secretary Kissinger had made such a decision. It was the result of a visit he had made to Latin America, where he found that the Foreign Service officers serving there were woefully ignorant of U.S. activities in the rest of the world. Kissinger said he could not believe that some officers hardly knew what NATO meant. Thus, he decided that everyone had to go to a new region upon the next scheduled transfer. Like everything else, the project was given a name: GLOP, "Global Outlook Program."

So, where was GLOP going to take me? My counselor asked if I would accept an assignment to the U.S. Embassy in Paris as political counselor, the number three in the hierarchy. I responded that I would think about it—for ten seconds. I accepted immediately. It was a dream assignment, especially for our bilingual family.

PHOTO GALLERY

50

1. Léopold Sédar Senghor, president of the Republic of Senegal, meeting in the Oval Office with President Jimmy Carter, March 1978. The author, then U.S. ambassador to Senegal, is to Senghor's left. Carter tried to persuade Senghor to boycott the Olympic Games scheduled to be held in Moscow in 1980. Senghor refused, reminding him that the United States had consistently argued against bringing politics into sports.

2. Secretary of State Edmund Muskie, meeting with Deputy Assistant Secretaries of State for Intelligence and Research Philip Stoddard (left) and the author (right), June 1980, during the Carter administration. Muskie, a former governor of the State of Maine, served as secretary of state for only nine months. He negotiated the release of fifty-two American citizens who had been held hostage by the Islamic revolutionary government of Iran.

3. Secretary of State Alexander Haig greeting the author at a State Department reception, September 1981. The author was then principal deputy assistant secretary in the Bureau of Intelligence and Research. Secretary Haig encouraged the bureau to find evidence that the Soviets were responsible for the failed attempt to assassinate Pope John Paul II in May 1981. The Italian government's investigation determined that the perpetrator acted alone.

To Suzanne and Herman Cohen
with best wishes,

Ronald Reagan   *Nancy Reagan*

4. The author (left), then senior director for Africa on the National Security Council, and his spouse Suzanne Cohen (right), with President and Mrs. Ronald Reagan prior to the state dinner in honor of President of the Republic of Congo Denis Sassou-Nguessou, April 1988. Three years earlier, in 1985, in the wake of the Iran-Contra scandal, Reagan made no public appearances for four months. He went public again in January 1986, beginning with a morning briefing about Mozambique from the author.

5. President Ronald Reagan meeting with Kenyan president Daniel Arap Moi in the Oval Office in May 1988. The author, as senior director for Africa on the National Security Council, is on the left taking notes. President Reagan persuaded President Moi to have multiparty elections rather than the "one-party state" that existed in the majority of African nations at the time.

6. The author was sworn in as assistant secretary of state for African Affairs by Secretary of State James A. Baker in April 1989 in the Benjamin Franklin official reception room on the eighth floor of the State Department's Truman Building.

7. The author, then assistant secretary of state for African Affairs, visiting Nigerian president Ibrahim Babangida in the capital city Lagos, August 1989. Babangida had taken power in a military coup after a democratic election in 1986. In 1993 General Sani Abacha seized power in another military coup. Shortly before ceding power in 1998, Abacha died of poison administered by a prostitute.

8.   President George H. W. Bush introducing South African president Nelson Mandela to the author, then assistant secretary of state for Africa, during his first official visit to the United States in April 1990. Mandela had been in prison for 27 years under the minority white "apartheid" regime. Despite his many years in prison, Mandela worked with his former jailers to promote national unity.

9

ASSIGNMENT PARIS UNDER KISSINGER'S SCRUTINY

As soon as school ended for the summer in June 1974, we arranged to rent our home, put our furniture in storage, and packed what we would need in Paris. We flew to Paris on United Airlines.

Upon arrival at Charles de Gaulle Airport, we were met by Johnnie Berg, the American Embassy's very busy greeter and guide. Most of his airport greeting work involved high-level visitors from the U.S. government, such as cabinet secretaries and members of the U.S. Congress, who traveled frequently to European capitals.

Johnnie took us to the Hotel Van Loo in the center of Paris. We would be staying there for about two weeks until my predecessor, Allen Holmes, moved out of the political counselor's apartment on the Avenue Kléber in the swanky 16th arrondissement (district). Alan was transferring to the U.S. Embassy in Rome.

Two weeks later we moved into the apartment at 87 Avenue Kléber, about a block away from the Trocadero circle. The flat was on the fourth floor of a five-story building with two apartments on each floor. When we went inside, we could not believe how large the apartment was—4,800 square feet, four times the amount of space as our house in Washington. Fortunately, it was fully furnished. We needed to supply the pictures for the walls, the dishes for our meals, and the sheets for our beds, but little else. The large bookcases were full of books. The living room had a full grand piano. Clearly, the apartment was meant for diplomatic entertaining. Suzanne and I, as the political counselor, were expected to do a considerable amount of entertaining of French diplomatic and other senior officials, as well as journalists and political personalities.

The first order of business was to purchase a family automobile.

We bought a Peugeot 504, one of the popular sedans in France with a reputation for good performance and easy maintenance. Both our apartment building and the American Embassy had parking spots reserved for us.

On my first day in the office, I was introduced to Ambassador John Irwin, who was gracious and welcoming. Irwin was a Nixon administration political appointee. His substantial fortune came from the IBM Corporation, where he was one of the founders together with the Watson family. He was married to a member of the Watson family.

My office at the Embassy was on a corner on the first floor up. On one side, I had a view of the Place de la Concorde. On the other side, I was across a narrow street from the luxurious Hotel Crillon. Behind me, on the wall, was a large painting with bullet holes in it from resistance fighters during World War II.

The Political Section had ten Foreign Service officers and four Foreign Service secretaries. Individual FSOs covered French policy toward Africa, the Middle East, Asia, Europe, the Soviet Union and Eastern Europe, the USA, and political-military affairs. There was a four-person unit that covered internal French politics, including a labor attaché who maintained contacts with France's substantial labor movement. My staff in the embassy political section was larger than the one in the State Department that covered all of francophone Central Africa.

During my first week on the job, I made an appointment to visit the French Foreign Ministry, also known as the Quai d'Orsay for its location next to the River Seine. My main purpose was to become acquainted with the French officials responsible for relations with the United States. Secondly, I wanted to discuss the issue of U.S. nuclear-powered naval vessels making visits to French ports. The French government was not authorizing these visits because of the danger of a nuclear accident. They were skeptical of our promise to pay for any repairs. The French wanted to see an insurance policy.

The diplomats on the American desk greeted me warmly and took me to pay a courtesy call on the third-ranking person in the ministry, Ambassador Emmanuel de Margerie, the political director. When I raised the issue of nuclear ship visits with him, he responded that Secretary of State Henry Kissinger was expected to visit two weeks later, and that issue was on the agenda for discussion.

After I returned to the Embassy, I told Ambassador Irwin about my conversation at the Foreign Ministry. When I mentioned Kissinger's impending visit, he became quite upset. Apparently, Kissinger had informed the French that he was coming but had failed to inform his own ambassador. Instead of giving himself time to cool off, he fired off an electronic "eyes only" message to Kissinger. "I don't think you need an ambassador here in Paris. You can deal directly with the French without even letting me know, etc...."

Kissinger responded with an apology. "Please forgive me. You were not informed because of the incompetence of my staff. It will not happen again."

Ambassador Irwin then departed on vacation to his ranch in Arizona. While Irwin was in Arizona, the White House announced the appointment of Deputy Secretary of State Kenneth Rush to be the new ambassador to France. Irwin returned to Paris to say his farewells. The first thing he said to me when he returned was, "Rush's appointment was Kissinger's way of responding to my complaint."

Irwin took me along on most of his farewell calls. I was impressed by the breadth of his contacts, including the leadership of the French Communist Party. He was clearly popular within the French political-diplomatic community.

Kenneth Rush's appointment as ambassador to France was also related to something he did to annoy Secretary Kissinger. Having breakfast at home one weekday morning in 1974, Kissinger was watching a news telecast. During a report on tensions in Cyprus, the news anchor announced that Deputy Secretary of State Kenneth Rush had agreed to discuss the issue and to talk about U.S. policy in the Aegean Sea subregion. Beyond Rush's actual remarks about the issue, Kissinger was furious that Rush had accepted the TV newscaster's invitation. He did not want his deputy appearing on TV to discuss U.S. policy. That job was Kissinger's alone.

At that moment, Washington was in a state of turmoil. President Nixon had just resigned because of the infamous Watergate scandal, and Vice President Gerald Ford had been sworn in as Nixon's replacement. Ford accepted Kissinger's recommendation to give Rush an ambassadorship to open the way for a more compatible deputy.

Kenneth Rush joined the Nixon administration in 1971 as ambassador to Germany. In that position, he helped negotiate the ground-breaking four-power agreement that ended the postwar crises over Berlin. Berlin became a city accessible to all travelers, and tensions between the NATO allies and the Soviet Union were greatly reduced. Rush was given significant credit for this diplomatic achievement.

Rush first met Nixon at Yale Law School, where Rush was a member of the faculty and Nixon was a student. Rush later joined the Union Carbide Corporation, where he rose to be president and CEO. Rush left Union Carbide to join the Nixon administration.

Within a day of his arrival in Paris, Ambassador Rush caused a problem with French security, who were assigned to guard the American ambassador twenty-four hours a day. Rush decided to walk to the Embassy from his residence every morning. It took ten minutes maximum. French security feared that some extremist would try to attack Rush out of lingering anger over previous U.S. policy toward French colonialism in Algeria and Vietnam. They wanted Rush to take the short ride to the Embassy in his armored car. Nevertheless, Rush insisted on walking, except during inclement weather.

During initial briefings, I told Rush that the Political Section was concentrating on liaison with the Foreign Ministry in a daily exchange of views on the major international issues of mutual interest. We would leave relations between the embassy and President Valéry Giscard d'Estaing and his ministers to Rush and his deputy chief of mission. I also told him that we would be making a special effort to get to know the top people in the leftwing opposition, known as the Socialist-Communist Programme commun (Common Programme), under the leadership of veteran politician François Mitterrand. He responded that he would be available to meet with, or give hospitality to, any of the left leadership whom we recommended, except of course, the Communist Party leadership.

During Ambassador Rush's tenure, US-French relations were essentially trouble-free. The issue of U.S. nuclear ship visits to

French ports was solved by an American government pledge to be the insurer of first and last resort. In short, the French were persuaded that the USG would pay for any nuclear damage caused by American nuclear ship visits. They had it in writing.

In 1975, President Giscard d'Estaing proposed that the major economic powers of the world get together at the summit to discuss profound reforms in economic policy. The resulting summit meeting in November 1975 in France included the heads of state or government of the U.S.A., the U.K., Germany, Italy, Japan, and France. As expected, this resulted in lots of work for the U.S. embassy staff.

The summit took place over a weekend at the Rambouillet Chateau, about thirty-five miles west of Paris. Each head of state had his own apartment suite within the chateau. My assignment was to make sure everything was OK in President Ford's suite. My first challenge was the president's bed, which was clearly too short for a six-foot-five-inch chief executive. The French staff arranged for a longer bed.

After President Ford's arrival, the French raised the issue of Sunday church services. They said that American Protestant clergy at the American Church of Paris were available to offer Ford a private service at the chateau. President Ford said he wanted to attend a church service but would prefer to go to a normal Sunday service at a neighborhood house of worship. This, of course, caused the security detail to become virtually hysterical. Imagine a U.S. president mingling with local citizens at a local church. Who knew what sort of evil people might be mingling with the crowd with the intention of harming the president?

That challenge required creative thinking. The nearest location was a Catholic church, about five miles from the chateau in the historic village of Montfort l'Amaury. We went to see the head priest, who said that the regular Sunday service was offered at 10 a.m. every week. He said President Ford would be welcome to participate.

After some brainstorming, we asked the priest if he could schedule a special service that would begin at 11 a.m. and be closed to the public. Instead, we would ask American embassy personnel to fill the pews. Indeed, on that Sunday, embassy employees, interested in seeing their president, flocked to the church and filled the pews. Accompanying President Ford to the church were the president of

France and the prime minister of Italy. My wife Suzanne and I were privileged to sit right behind them.

This first-ever economic summit ran smoothly. A final communiqué was issued pledging cooperation in bringing economic development to the poor countries. The economic summit became institutionalized and held annually. As time went on, attendance at the economic summits increased considerably, as every significant trading nation was determined not to miss out.

In late 1975, President Giscard d'Estaing was invited to give a speech in Lafayette, Louisiana, the heart of French culture in the United States. Preparation for this event greatly increased discussions between the embassy and the French bureaucracy.

At one point during the preparations, I recalled to the president's advisers the disaster that took place a decade earlier when President Charles de Gaulle paid an official visit to Canada. During his stop in Montréal, he spoke to a crowd from the balcony of city hall and ended his speech with the declaration "Vive le Québec Libre!" ("Long live Free Quebec)." In other words, he was expressing support for the militant Quebec independence movement, which was extremely vocal at the time. This was totally unacceptable to the Canadian government, and de Gaulle was asked to cut his visit short and return to France prematurely. This led me to urge the president's advisers to make sure that Giscard did not proclaim, "Vive la Louisiane libre!"

While U.S.-French relations were quite smooth during Ambassador Rush's tenure, U.S. relations with the French political opposition became quite rocky because of Secretary Kissinger's concern that the French left might be elected to power in partnership with the French Communist Party. Having Communist ministers in the government of a NATO member was totally unacceptable to Kissinger.

The embassy pushed back against the secretary's apprehensions. We argued that the status of the once-powerful French Communist Party was degraded by its minority position alongside the majority Socialist Party within the Programme commun. The communists had become a minority party, with only 13 percent of the vote, compared to the 25 percent it had once enjoyed. We argued that the communists were in decline.

Despite our arguments, Kissinger issued a directive that the embassy approach the leadership of the Socialist Party and demand that they sever their partnership with the Communist Party. We knew they would be coming to power eventually, and it would be unacceptable to see communist ministers in a NATO government.

When the directive came in, Ambassador Rush held a meeting with me and Deputy Chief of Mission Sam Gammon. We agreed that the action Kissinger was demanding would constitute blatant interference in French internal affairs. The French press would have a field day attacking the American "imperialists."

Since I traveled outside of Paris about once a month to talk to provincial political leaders and was scheduled for a visit to Marseilles, the port city in the south, I had an opportunity to carry out Secretary Kissinger's directive. The mayor of Marseilles, Gaston Deferre, also happened to be the Socialist Party's foreign affairs chief. So, I volunteered to carry out Kissinger's directive with him. Both the ambassador and DCM Gammon were happy to hand the ball over to me.

Deferre received me graciously. He told me that visits from American embassy officials were rare. Deferre was quite open about French politics and gave me a significant amount of new information. I saved the tough job for the end, explaining Kissinger's apprehensions about the Communists potentially becoming ministers after a Programme commun electoral victory, which appeared inevitable. The United States government was officially requesting that the Communist Party be ejected from the Socialist Party coalition.

After I finished, it was clear that the mayor had become furious. First, he was upset about our interference in French internal affairs from the level of the American secretary of state. That was bad enough. But even worse, the Americans were doubting the ability of the French Socialists to "handle" the Communists or keep them from causing problems.

He told me the story of the immediate aftermath of World War II. Along with other French resistance fighters, he had returned to Marseilles to find city hall occupied by members of the French Communist Party and proceeded to call out the roughest members of the French truck drivers' union. The communists were gone within a matter of days. "We know how to handle communists a lot better than you Americans," he said, as he ushered me out somewhat contemptuously.

Returned to Paris, I reported to Ambassador Rush, who sent a note to Kissinger to say that we tried and failed to persuade the Socialists that the republic would be in danger if they came to power with communists.

Nothing more happened on this subject until three months later, when Mayor Deferre was on an election campaign stop in the city of Bordeaux. During one of his public speeches, he had a burst of nationalism and told the story of my earlier visit, in words filled with indignation and contempt.

I first heard about Deferre's speech on a Sunday afternoon at my apartment. Inundated by telephone calls, I refused to comment. But it was clear that we had a public relations problem. The following Wednesday, the French satirical weekly, *Le Canard Enchaîné* (The Chained Duck) ran a cartoon of me dressed as a gun-toting cowboy. The caption read, "The American cowboy descends on Marseilles."

The scandal lasted in the press for a few days before fading. But then, something extraordinary happened. The *New York Times* bureau chief in Paris called me to say, "Did you know that you are now the darling of the French political right?" And the invitations poured in. Suzanne and I had many a dinner at great French restaurants as guests of the various right-wing political parties. I had the distinct feeling that Ambassador Rush was a bit jealous.

In November 1976, Democratic governor Jimmy Carter of Georgia won the presidential election, defeating incumbent Gerald Ford. Between the election and Carter's inauguration, scheduled for January 1977, Vice President–Elect Walter Mondale traveled to the main NATO partners to assure them there would be no change in U.S. policy toward the collective defense. During his visit to Paris, he totally ignored Ambassador Rush and the rest of us in the embassy, clearly wanting a total break with the Ford administration.

Rush remained in his position as ambassador until March 1977, when he was replaced by Ambassador Arthur Hartman, a career Foreign Service officer. About that time, President Carter nominated me to be ambassador to the Republic of Senegal in West Africa.

After lots of paperwork and Senate confirmation, the family and I packed up and departed Paris for Dakar, Senegal, in September 1977.

Several years later, in 1981, Socialist Party leader François Mitterrand was elected president of France. His government included three French Communist ministers. By the end of Mitterrand's term, the Communist Party had become a mere shadow of its previous self. The embassy's prediction in 1975 proved accurate.

10

AMBASSADOR TO SENEGAL

In March 1977, we received a visit in Paris from Ambassador William Schauffele, the assistant secretary of state for Africa. Bill was one of the most senior Africa experts in the U.S. government at that time.

He told me that I was being considered for an ambassadorship in Africa, and the choice was between Senegal and Upper Volta (later changed to Burkina Faso). With no hesitation I expressed my preference for Senegal, which was the political and intellectual leader of French West Africa. Senegal's president, Léopold Senghor, had a worldwide reputation as a serious and consequential statesman.

President Carter sent my nomination to be ambassador to Senegal to the Senate Foreign Relations Committee in May 1977. I went to Washington for the confirmation hearings, consultations with various bureaus and agencies, and the purchase of necessary items for Africa. During my consultations, it was clear that we were depending on President Senghor to influence other African governments on a variety of issues, including UN resolutions.

The committee hearings were without difficulties. Most of the senators had met me during their visits to Paris. I spent about two weeks consulting with the various agencies. The under secretary for management presided over my swearing-in ceremony. I was happy to have my mother, brother, and other relatives come to Washington from New York for the event.

While I was in Washington, the U.S. embassy in Dakar sent me a summary of how diplomatic work was carried out in that country. They instructed me to make sure to bring a formal morning-coat outfit for my presentation of credentials to President Senghor, who was a traditionalist when it came to ceremonials.

I went to a rental store in downtown Washington that did a big business in morning-coat outfits. They were astonished when I told them I wanted to buy one, rather than rent it. The salesman said to me, "You are the first person I have seen who wants to buy the outfit." During my three years in Senegal, I wore that morning coat for ceremonies quite a few times, mainly during visits of foreign heads of state.

Back in Paris in July for goodbyes and packing, we remained until early September, when my predecessor as political counselor, Allen Holmes, arrived. During August, we managed to squeeze in a family vacation in southern France.

We arrived in Dakar during the second week of September and went straight to the ambassador's residence after greeting staff members who came to the airport. The Residence was in an ideal location, situated on a hill overlooking the bay of Dakar and the ocean beyond. The Residence was also quite beautiful, with elegant furniture and a full-sized swimming pool.

But the bad news we learned upon arrival was that, because of faulty construction, the Residence was literally coming apart and becoming dangerous to live in. The kitchen was already in a separate structure about fifty feet from the main house. We had no choice but to look for a new home, knowing that nothing could be as nice as the existing one.

One of the problems involved in looking for a new embassy residence was the competition. While the United States has a policy of establishing an embassy in virtually every independent nation, other governments have one ambassador covering five other countries in the same region. In west Africa, Dakar was the place that governments established embassies that covered multiple countries.

After a year of looking at various options, without finding anything suitable, we discovered a house under construction by a private person, located on the seashore in a diplomatic neighborhood. We negotiated a ten-year lease. In return, he agreed to make changes in the construction plan to make the house more adaptable to the entertainment and other needs of an ambassador's residence. It was still not as good as the original, but it was not bad.

My presentation of credentials was quite ceremonial and routine. There was an exchange of speeches expressing US-Senegal friendship and cooperation, followed by a reception. What was most interesting was the private conversation that President Senghor and I had at the end.

Senghor told me that the Palestine Liberation Organization (PLO) had been authorized to establish an office in Dakar. Since 95 percent of the Senegalese are Muslim, the government could not do anything less. There was no Israeli embassy, because almost all the African governments had severed relations with Israel immediately after the 1973 Sinai war.

By way of assurance, Senghor said that Senegal and Israel maintained political relations through the annual meetings of the Socialist International. Also, Israeli foreign minister Shimon Peres was a regular informal visitor to Dakar.

To make me feel even better, Senghor said, "Mr. Ambassador, you should know that I have Jewish blood in my family. My first wife was a French lady whose mother was Jewish. Therefore, my two sons have Jewish blood." Senghor himself, was a devout Roman Catholic, who arose at 5 a.m. every morning to read the Bible in Latin.

The American Embassy in Dakar was somewhat larger than others in West Africa, because several U.S. agencies had their regional offices there. These included Commerce, Agriculture, Federal Aviation, Internal Revenue, and Defense. Defense had both an intelligence attaché and a cooperation team that worked with the Senegalese army. During my first meeting with all the agency reps and the senior embassy section chiefs, I warned that I would not tolerate turf fights.

My deputy chief of mission was Fred Galanto, a highly experienced Foreign Service officer who was quite knowledgeable about the Middle East.

The American School of Dakar accepted our two sons. The school was established by Protestant missionaries, who had stations throughout West Africa. It served as a boarding school for the missionary children whose parents were working in interior villages. The teachers were all Americans, who were there for periods of up to five years.

Our sons were quite comfortable at the American School. One day, our younger son Alain, then in the fourth grade, came home to say that he had caused a disturbance when he expressed his belief in evolution, contrary to the fundamentalist belief in creation. It was a minor issue that passed quickly.

The American School went only to the eighth grade. After that, the missionary students transferred to the American School of Kinshasa in the Republic of Zaire (now the Democratic Republic of the Congo). Our older son Marc completed the eighth grade during our second year in Dakar. For the third year, his only other option was to go to the French lycée Jean Mermoz. Since he was bilingual, he was comfortable there, except for math. He found the French system different and hard to understand. We hired a tutor who helped him integrate into the French math curriculum.

At the lycée, Marc discovered the overall French system. The teacher lectured, and the students took notes. There was no discussion. Marc asked his teachers if discussions could be allowed. Since he was the son of the American ambassador, the teachers decided to give it a try. But they insisted that Marc organize the discussions, which he did.

Because Marc was so comfortable in the French system, he continued his high school studies at the French International School of Washington, along with younger brother Alain, after our return there in 1980.

Ambassadorial life in Senegal was relatively calm. There was an absence of crisis interspersed with some interesting moments.

One evening in 1978, at 11:30 p.m., I received a call from the State Department Operations Center, the watch office that monitors events worldwide twenty-four hours a day, seven days a week. It briefs the secretary of state every morning, and keeps all other senior officials informed.

This call was about three U.S. Air Force transport aircraft that were bringing French troops from Corsica to the southern Congo, locale of an ongoing invasion of so-called Katangan Gendarmes coming from Angola, with Angolan government support. The invaders were Congolese rebels opposing the Congolese government of President Mobutu, who was supporting the UNITA rebels against the Angolan government. As the aircraft needed to refuel at the Dakar airport, I was instructed to obtain the Senegalese government's authorization. The aircraft were scheduled to arrive "three hours from now."

So I called my neighbor, Prime Minister Abdou Diouf, who asked me about the purpose of the mission. I told him it was to help President Mobutu fight an invasion supported by the Angolan government. He promptly responded: "If it is to help Mobutu, we agree. I will call the airport immediately."

The next morning at the airport, the American C-5 Galaxy aircraft were on the ground. I had never seen such giant airplanes. They had tanks and artillery inside, as well as several hundred French troops. The Senegalese government arranged to send two hundred troops to join the mission. I asked the mission commander if he could stop in Senegal for a few days on the way back. I wanted to open the aircraft to the Senegalese people for public tours as a gesture of friendly U.S-Senegal relations. He said he would arrange it.

Early in 1978, the family and I traveled to the Gambia for the presentation of my credentials as the U.S. ambassador. The Gambia is a tiny country that straddles the Gambia River in the heart of Senegal, effectively cutting Senegal in half. From Gambia's independence from the UK in 1960 until 1980, the U.S. ambassador to Senegal had dual accreditation as ambassador to the Gambia. We had an embassy in Banjul, the capital city, under the leadership of a chargé d'affaires. After my departure in 1980, the United States started assigning fulltime ambassadors to the Gambia.

How did this strange geographic relationship between the Gambia and Senegal come about? During the nineteenth century, when the Europeans colonized most of Africa, the British concentrated on exploring river valleys. They settled in the Gambia River valley, while the French took territory on both flanks, in Senegal. In 1935, the French and the UK agreed on an exchange of territory. The French would take over the Gambia, to be incorporated into Senegal, while the British would take over the French territory of Gabon. But the proposed exchange was interrupted by World War II and never took place.

My presentation of credentials in the Gambia was fascinating. Because of Muslim tradition, my wife was not invited to the ceremony, but my two sons, Marc age 15, and Alain age 11, were allowed to attend. My wife was invited to tea with the First Lady.

The official presidential vehicle called for us at the U.S. Embassy at 2 p.m. It was a supersized Bentley that must have been built in the 1920s. It had a convertible roof that disappeared completely so that the populace could have a good look at the occupants with the windows rolled down. The crowds were large and cheering, both coming and going.

During my private conversation with President Jawara, the main topic of conversation concerned the issue of constructing a bridge across the Gambia River. In the absence of a bridge, vehicles were forced to wait as much as four days to go by ferry from one part of Senegal to the other. This increased the cost of supplies to consumers.

I emphasized to Jawara that international financial support was available to build a bridge, which he opposed. What was needed, he said, was not a bridge but a vehicle roadway on top of a dam that would prevent intrusive salt water from moving upstream during the dry season, thereby causing difficulties with agriculture. I told him that I would explore that idea.

Afterwards, during one of my periodic meetings with Senegal's president Senghor, I raised the issue of a Gambian River crossing. Senghor told me that he was becoming fed up with Jawara's delay and had decided to build a road around the Gambia whose eastern boundary was inside Senegal. Before my assignment in Dakar ended, the road was completed. Senegalese and other vehicles that did not want to wait for the ferry were making the road trip in about four hours.

In 1978, President Carter decided to send his mother, Lilian Carter, age 85, on a goodwill trip to West Africa. She was accompanied by an aide and a State Department medical doctor. Senegal and the Gambia were her first two stops. Both her visits turned out to be highly popular, because she was such a vivacious, uninhibited, and charming lady.

During Mrs. Carter's visit with President Senghor, he asked her about her time as a Peace Corps volunteer in India, when she was 65 years old. She told Senghor that she had worked on a family planning project in India, and that he would appreciate how vicious the press could be. She explained that her son Jimmy, the governor of the State of Georgia at the time, was ridiculed by an *Atlanta Journal* headline that read: "Governor Carter's mother is in India distributing condoms while her son is doing just the opposite." The headline referred to Governor and Mrs. Carter's having multiple infant children.

President Senghor was so captivated by Mrs. Carter's stories that he said at the end, "Mrs. Carter, you should write a book."

In the Gambia, stop number two, the reception, was more formal. President Jawara gave a luncheon and a dinner in Mrs. Carter's honor. Both were quite lavish.

At the luncheon, Mrs. Carter was presented with a presidential gift, a heavy gold bracelet. She called me over to look at it, saying, "Mr. Ambassador, what do you think this is worth?" I said, "Miss Lilian, I believe this bracelet is worth ninety-nine dollars." Her response was, "If I keep this bracelet, the press will destroy my son Jimmy."

At the dinner, the president's spouse, the First Lady, was not the same person as at the lunch. Mrs. Carter was confused until I told her about polygamy under the Muslim religion.

In December 1979, the Soviet army invaded Afghanistan, whose communist government had been overthrown by Islamist rebels. The Soviets saw this revolution as a danger to themselves. The Soviet army's intrusion into Afghanistan enraged President Carter, who saw it as naked, unjustified aggression. It dominated Carter's foreign policy until the end of his term.

One obvious way to punish the Soviets involved the summer Olympic games scheduled to be held in Moscow during the summer of 1980. President Carter declared that the United States would be boycotting the games and asked all other nations to do the same.

Africa's fifty-four nations were clearly seen as potential boycotters. Large, strong nations should not be allowed to invade small nations with impunity. To persuade African governments to follow the American example, President Carter sent Muhammad Ali, the heavyweight boxing champion, on a tour of ten African nations. The last stop on his tour was Senegal.

Ali's four-day visit to Dakar was an absolute sensation. The Senegalese loved him. The first afternoon, about fifty women with babies lined up at my residence to present their children to him. The children were all named Muhammad Ali. He patiently took each child, kissed it, and gave each mother fifty dollars.

Boxing is a major sport in Senegal. During his first evening in Dakar, Ali was happy to appear at the boxing matches in the arena. At one point, he was invited into the ring. He put on a pair of boxing gloves and began sparring with Senegalese boxers. With each one he pretended to be knocked out and went down on the floor. The crowd became hysterical.

Ali's mission was to persuade the Senegalese to boycott the 1980 Olympic games in Moscow. In that respect his mission failed. None of the African governments, including Senegal, agreed to the boycott. They kept repeating to Ali that it is usually the United States who preaches against politicizing international sports.

The last event for Muhammad Ali was a family lunch at President Senghor's beach house about thirty miles south of Dakar. My wife and I were the only other Americans invited.

Toward the end of the lunch, President Senghor came close to Ali and whispered in his ear. They both got up and walked out of the room together, returning about twenty minutes later.

As is customary in these diplomatic events, toasts were offered to signal the occasion's end. In his toast, President Senghor talked about the excellent relations between Senegal and the United States. Muhammad Ali's toast lauded the Senegalese for their wonderful hospitality and enthusiasm for him. He also had a special word of praise for President Senghor. He said: "Senegal was the only country in Africa that I visited where the head of state himself personally took me to the bathroom."

During the month of June 1980, I was completing my three-year assignment as U.S. ambassador to Senegal and the Gambia. Our family effects were all packed and ready for shipment to Washington. We had finished a round of farewell dinners given by fellow ambassadors and government officials. We were about to depart when, at the last minute, we received an instruction from the State Department to delay. Vice President Walter Mondale had scheduled a goodwill visit to several West African nations in mid-July, with Senegal the first stop. I had to be there to manage his visit.

Mondale arrived at Dakar International Airport on Air Force Two early on a Tuesday morning. His wife and teenage son accompanied him, along with members of his staff and Secret Service protectors. I boarded the aircraft to welcome Mondale. He was most gracious in his response and asked me to come to his hotel at 3 p.m. that day after he and his party had gotten over their jet lag.

When I went to Mondale's hotel suite at the appointed time of 3 p.m., I found him in his shirt, tie, and underwear shorts, as his valet was pressing his trousers. He was quite relaxed as we went over his schedule of appointments and social events. His wife had a separate schedule focused on women's organizations.

I returned to the Embassy for an hour prior to Mondale's first meeting with the Senegalese minister of foreign affairs. There, I had to deal with a minor crisis. The head of the Secret Service detail came to tell me that none of his men could speak French and none of the Senegalese security team could speak English. They could not communicate. I asked if he would accept my son Marc, then sixteen years old and bilingual in English and French. The answer was a resounding yes, with the addition that Marc would be paid an interpreter's salary.

That first afternoon, Mondale had time for just two meetings, with the minister of foreign affairs and the president of the National Assembly. In both conversations, Mondale stressed President Jimmy Carter's strong feelings of friendship for Senegalese President Léopold Senghor and the U.S. government's high regard for Senegal's democratic form of government. He did not bring any proposals for new projects in economic development.

That first evening, my son Marc had dinner with Mondale's son. After Marc returned home, he had an announcement for his parents. "Tomorrow, they are going to give me a gun," he boasted. Needless to say, our instantaneous response was, "Absolutely no gun."

The following day, Wednesday, Mondale had substantive meetings with President Senghor and other political leaders, including those in the opposition. He was particularly fascinated with Senghor's views on Africa's cultural constraints on democracy. Senghor also assured Mondale that Senegal was solidly pro-Israel, despite the fact that the Senegalese population was 95 percent Muslim.

Riding between appointments in the ambassador's limousine, Mondale and I became relaxed and friendly. At one point, he spoke about the presidential election scheduled for that November. He told me that President Carter would be defeated for reelection by the Republican candidate, who had not yet been formally selected but who would likely be Ronald Reagan.

On Wednesday evening, my wife Suzanne and I hosted a large reception at the Residence, with the guests gathered around the swimming pool in the back patio. As the guests started to arrive and photographers were snapping pictures, Mondale whispered in my ear, "Tell them I do not want to be photographed with a drink in my hand." That must have been said with the folks back home in Minnesota in mind.

Among the tourist destinations in Senegal, Mondale spent some time on Gorée Island, where slaves from West African nations departed for the United States. Gorée is the most important tourist stop for American visitors.

After three days and three nights in Senegal, Vice President Mondale had accomplished a great deal. Of especial importance, Mondale's in-depth knowledge of Africa and its development issues made an excellent impression on the Senegalese elites whom he met. Above all, his good humor and modesty caused everyone to relax and think good things about the USA.

After Mondale's departure, I jokingly told my ambassadorial colleagues that, since I had remained an extra month, they should offer a new round of farewell dinners.

We departed Dakar the last week of July and headed directly for Washington, where I was assigned as principal deputy assistant secretary in the Bureau of Intelligence and Research, an entirely new brief. Though I had been reading intelligence my entire career, this assignment involved the production of intelligence and the supervision of an entire bureau of intelligence analysts. It sounded dull but turned out to be quite exciting.

11

THE INTELLIGENCE COMMUNITY

Arriving in Washington in late July 1980, we took advantage of the State Department's policy of financing two months in temporary quarters for Foreign Service employees while they arranged permanent lodging for their Washington assignments. For our temporary lodgings we rented a two-bedroom apartment in the Bristol House on Pennsylvania Avenue downtown. Having informed the tenant in our Georgetown house that we were returning and that she and her family should depart, we immediately started some planned renovations.

My Washington assignment was as principal deputy assistant secretary in the Bureau of Intelligence and Research. Assistant Secretary Ronald Spiers, one of the most respected senior officers in the Foreign Service, had selected me.

The Bureau of Intelligence and Research, commonly referred to as INR, is one of sixteen U.S. intelligence agencies. In 1980, the director of the Central Intelligence also headed the entire intelligence community as DCI, director of central intelligence. The Clinton administration created the position of director of national intelligence, DNI, to supervise the entire community, including the CIA.

While I had been a regular consumer of intelligence products throughout my career, this was my first experience in the production and distribution of analytical intelligence. The INR Bureau has a twenty-four-hour watch office that makes sure vital intelligence is rapidly distributed to senior State Department officials. The bureau prepares a daily morning briefing for the secretary of state, who receives it at home before breakfast. INR represents the State Department on the National Intelligence Council, which prepares national estimates on important issues for the president and senior national security officials in all agencies.

When I arrived at INR, the corps of analysts was about equally divided between career Foreign Service officers, who spent three years looking at specific countries and regions, and career civil servants, who spent decades looking at specific regions. I found that the arrangement worked quite well, with both groups providing their own expertise and experience to the mix.

Unsurprisingly, I had some interesting experiences dealing with the intelligence analysts, the intelligence consumers, and the other intelligence agencies.

In January 1981, the newly elected Reagan administration took office. The new CIA director, William Casey, was active in Long Island politics and was a good friend of my late first cousin Harry Minkoff, a financial supporter of the Republican Party in the northern Long Island Kings Point area.

President Reagan's first secretary of state, retired general Alexander Haig, had been President Nixon's chief of staff and NATO supreme commander. Haig was also a fervent "Cold Warrior" and wanted the INR assistant secretary to prove that the Soviets were behind the attempted assassination of Pope John Paul II in April 1981, after Assistant Secretary Spiers had left the bureau to become the U.S. ambassador to Pakistan. To fill the vacancy, Haig selected his old acquaintance, senior CIA officer Hugh Montgomery.

When Montgomery took over as INR assistant secretary, he told me that he would be spending much of his time in Rome searching for the Soviet connection to the attempted assassination of the pope. He had served in Rome as CIA station chief and knew the right people. In view of his concentration on that one issue, he said, I would be running INR from day to day.

Secretary Haig had a regular 8:30 a.m. senior staff meeting with the State Department under secretaries, with no representatives of the geographic bureaus. He also wanted the head of INR to be there. Because of Montgomery's many absences in Rome, I attended most of Haig's morning meetings. As the regional bureaus were not represented, I took it upon myself to mention two or three of the most important overnight events in the regions. Haig grew to appreciate that. At one staff meeting, when my turn came, I said, "Nothing to report." Haig looked at me in disbelief and asked, "What, no homilies today?"

My big adventure with Secretary Haig involved the ten-day Falklands war that began on April 2, 1982. On March 30, an INR officer from the watch came to my office with an urgent matter. He showed me a piece of paper he had torn off a teletype machine. It said, "Arriving at the Malvinas in 72 hours." When I asked him what it was all about, he replied that the message was from the commander of Argentina's fleet, indicating they would be invading the British Falkland Islands within the next seventy-two hours.

This was the first piece of intelligence indicating that the Argentine government had decided to use force to take over the Falklands, which the Argentines called the Malvinas. During the previous months there had been a lot of rhetoric from Buenos Aires threatening to use force if the U.K. refused to negotiate a transfer of ownership. But none of the intelligence agencies had predicted an actual invasion.

I rushed upstairs to Secretary Haig's office to give him the news. He became quite agitated and declared, "They are too far away. There is no way we can stop them." Throughout the U.S. government, overwhelming sentiment developed to support the British in the war. Haig, however, felt there was still time to negotiate and proposed that course of action to the president. But Haig was a minority of one. His most vocal opponent was Ambassador Jeane Kirkpatrick, the U.S. permanent representative to the United Nations, who wanted to support the ultra-right-wing Argentine regime. Haig's reluctance to act expeditiously in support of the British effectively ended his career as secretary of state.

After the end of the Falklands war, in which the British enjoyed a big victory, I wanted to find out why we did not learn of Argentina's intentions until seventy-two hours before the invasion started. As noted above, for several months prior to the war, the Argentine government had been threatening: "If the UK refuses to negotiate, we will use force." Every U.S. government intelligence agency had a representative in Buenos Aires. Why hadn't they predicted what happened? What I discovered was that nobody believed Argentina would actually carry out their threat. Basically, civilized nations do not do that sort of thing.

In July 1982, George P. Shultz, president of the Bechtel Corporation, replaced Haig as secretary of state, a position he held until the end of Reagan's presidency in 1989. During Shultz's first two years in office, I continued in my position at INR and thus had regular contacts with him. Shultz had previous cabinet-level experience as secretary of the Treasury, secretary of labor, and director of the Office of Management and Budget. It did not take him long to learn about the Reagan administration's priorities.

During the period 1982–1984, a major challenge for U.S. foreign policy was the Central American government of Nicaragua, which had come under the control of a Marxist-Leninist regime led by a political grouping known as the Sandinistas. In Cold War terms, the Sandinistas were ideologically aligned with the Soviet Union. While Secretary Haig was in office, the Sandinistas were almost an obsession for him. He could not believe that we had not found a nonmilitary way to force them out of power.

What annoyed Secretary Haig even more was that none of our Western allies seemed to care about the Sandinistas. He sent me on a visit to several countries in Western Europe to give my counterparts intelligence briefings about the Sandinistas, especially about their support for Marxist insurgents in El Salvador. What troubled Haig was the prospective conquest of Central American countries by Sandinista surrogates in El Salvador, Honduras, and eventually even Mexico. He could not believe it when I returned from my trip and reported that our friends in Britain, Belgium, the Netherlands, and Sweden did not see the Sandinistas as a great danger.

Determined not to give up, Haig instructed me to organize an intelligence community estimate on Mexico's capability to resist a Sandinista effort at subversion in the event they were to take over neighboring Guatemala. For this, he had the enthusiastic support of CIA director William Casey, who brought an experienced expert on Mexico out of retirement to direct the exercise. This "Mexican Estimate" became a critically important effort by the Cold War crowd to escalate tensions in the Western Hemisphere.

The final meeting of the National Intelligence Council to discuss the Mexico situation and vote on an assessment occurred in February 1974. I represented INR. CIA director Casey chaired the meeting. He went around the room counterclockwise, asking each agency representative to give an opinion. Seated at his immediate left, I would be the last to speak.

All of the agency representatives expressed the view that there was absolutely no danger of Mexico being subverted by Marxists who might gain power in neighboring Guatemala and El Salvador. Among this group was Director Casey's own CIA head of intelligence analysis. When it was my turn, I expressed the agreement of State Department/INR with the consensus. Mexico would not be in danger of Marxist subversion.

My statement made Casey really unhappy. He said that he was totally astonished that I, Hank Cohen, did not see what he could see. Mexico would be in grave danger in the event neighboring Guatemala were to fall under Marxist control. He was determined to do the exercise all over again, which he did after my departure from INR in 1974.

12

Personnel Management

In 1984, it was time to move on from the intelligence community. My old boss, Ron Spiers, had returned from Pakistan to become the under secretary for management and suggested that I take the position of principal deputy assistant secretary in the Office of the Director General of the Foreign Service. In that position, I would also have the title, director of personnel. The director general at that time was Ambassador Roy Atherton, the State Department's leading authority on the Middle East.

I accepted the position, feeling that it was one way of giving back for the great assignments I had enjoyed over the years.

The main work of the State Department's Director General's Office is the assignment process, rotating several thousand Foreign Service personnel to new jobs abroad and in Washington every few years. My job was mainly to handle problems in this complex process. The director general focused on overall policy, covering the Departments of State, Agriculture, and Commerce, as well as US-AID and several defense agencies.

Within the State Department, annual selection boards decided on promotions for Foreign Service officers. They also assigned low ranks to those with relatively mediocre performances as a basis for their being "selected out" of the Foreign Service, a process resulting in an annual set of hardship cases and controversy.

Of great significance in the promotion process is the threshold from midlevel to senior officer. After a certain number of years midlevel officers have to win promotion to senior officer or leave the service. The rank of senior officer in the Foreign Service is the equivalent of general or admiral in the military. New senior officers begin as Counselors, or one star. The next level is Minister, or two stars, followed by Minister Counselor, or three stars. The highest rank is Career Ambassador, or four stars. There are only two or three promotions to Career Ambassador each year.

Midlevel officers decide when they will compete for senior officer. They have three chances to win this promotion. If they fail, they must leave the service.

One of the most important responsibilities of the director of personnel is to negotiate with the American Foreign Service Association (AFSA), the officially accredited labor union representing all Foreign Service personnel, about working conditions, including assignments and promotions.

The Foreign Service has a grievance system. Any individual who feels that he or she has been treated unfairly can file a grievance. To resolve the grievance at the lowest possible level, AFSA works with the grievance officer in the Personnel Office. As director of personnel, I reviewed every grievance decision. I was also final decision maker for every grievance that could not be resolved at lower levels. There were not many of these.

What is unique about the Foreign Service personnel system is that the service administers its own personnel management. In the federal Civil Service, with two million employees, there is a centralized system covering all other government agencies through the Office of Personnel Management. Foreign Service officers and support staff serve in the Departments of State, Commerce, Agriculture, and USAID and are managed separately from the governmentwide civil service system. Instead, they are under the jurisdiction of the Director General of the Foreign Service, a senior Foreign Service officer who is usually a former ambassador.

During my time as principal deputy assistant secretary for personnel, I quite naturally witnessed some interesting personal dramas.

I remember receiving an officer who wanted to appeal his assignment to the American Embassy in Uganda as the person in charge of general services, which included office space, transportation, utilities, and employee housing. The officer requested that I cancel his assignment to Uganda. As he was uniquely qualified for the job and I considered it a pleasant environment, having served in that embassy myself, I asked for his reason. He responded, "If I transfer to Uganda, my wife will divorce me."

That very grave response led me to go back to the assignments people to ask if he was the only qualified person available for the Uganda position. Informed that he was the only available officer who had the particular skill set required, I had to deny his appeal. So, he was transferred to Uganda.

Years later, while traveling in Africa as assistant secretary of state, I saw this same officer at the American Embassy in Ouagadougou, Republic of Burkina Faso. I asked him to tell me about his Uganda experience. He said, "My wife divorced me."

In another case, an officer was being transferred from Warsaw to Zurich, via home leave in the States. Rather than accompany him, his British wife preferred to go to her family in London to wait for him there with the children. At the end of home leave, the officer stopped in London en route to Zurich. However, he informed his wife that he was leaving her and the children in London. He did not want them with him in Zurich.

He departed for Zurich on his own and reported for duty at the U.S. Consulate General. Back in London, his wife was not accepting his decision. She used the airline tickets she had for herself and the children to travel to Zurich and checked the family into a Zurich hotel. She sent the bills to the Consulate General, claiming the temporary lodging allowance available to all new arrivals for two months. Meanwhile, her husband had moved into regular housing, which made the situation untenable. When the problem came to me, I had no choice but to terminate his assignment and bring them all back to Washington.

With a service that has over ten thousand officers and staff, I was pleased that problems such as these two were not that frequent. At the end of my assignment to the Office of the Director General of the Foreign Service, I realized how important it was that we administered our own complex personnel system and were not under the jurisdiction of the OPM.

13

NATIONAL SECURITY COUNCIL UNDER PRESIDENT REAGAN

In late 1986, I had completed two full years in the Bureau of Personnel and was beginning to think of retirement and the possibility of a second career in foreign affairs with another employer. In July, I was invited to interview for the job of Dean of the School of International Affairs at the University of Denver. I spent three days there meeting with faculty and students and looking at life in the city. In the end, the job went to the acting dean who was a long-term member of the faculty.

In November, an event at the highest level of the U.S. government—the Iran-Contra scandal—created quite a stir in Washington. It involved the Central American nation of Nicaragua, which had fallen under the control of Marxist politicians. As they had done in 1975 in Angola, the Congress enacted legislation prohibiting the U.S. government from taking any military or related action in Nicaragua.

Within the National Security Council (NSC) there was a senior director who thought he had devised a way to circumvent this prohibition. His name was Oliver North, an Army lieutenant colonel. The people he wanted to help in Nicaragua were a right-wing insurgent militia known as the Contras, who had begun a guerrilla operation against the Marxist regime. North devised a scheme that took him on a trip to the then-friendly regime of the Shah of Iran, whom he persuaded to provide arms to the Contras. It was that simple.

But before the plan could be implemented, the story was leaked to the American press. The key congressional committee chairpersons were outraged. President Reagan had no other option but to fire both Oliver North and his boss, National Security Advisor Admiral John Poindexter. Because Reagan had advance awareness of the scheme, Reagan decided to lie low for a while, avoiding public appearances and public statements.

Reagan selected Frank Carlucci as the new national security advisor. A retired senior Foreign Service officer, Carlucci had been ambassador to Portugal in 1975, when a group of young army officers deposed the fascist regime of Antonio Salazar. Carlucci played an important role in Portugal's transition to democracy. At the time of his appointment as national security advisor in November 1986, he was working as the president and CEO of Sears Worldwide.

Carlucci's first decision as national security advisor was a bombshell. He fired the entire NSC staff, most of whom had absolutely no involvement with Iran-Contra, because he wanted to select all his senior directors. As his deputy, Carlucci named Col. Colin Powell, an army officer he had seen and admired in the Pentagon.

Before Carlucci's first day as national security advisor, set for January 1, 1987, he spent the month of December 1986 selecting his new staff of directors. During that period, Carlucci invited me to a conversation at his Sears office for the purpose of inviting me to be his senior director for Africa. When it was clear that we were on the same wavelength with respect to policy, I accepted his offer to take over the Africa portfolio. For the job of assistant director for Africa, some of my friends in USAID recommended Alison Rosenberg, USAID's policy director for Africa. After an interview, I offered her the position and she accepted. She was an invaluable partner for me in the African directorate in view of her vast experience in economic development. Also, because of my many absences on overseas travel, she represented the directorate with distinction on a daily basis.

I started at the NSC the first week in January 1987. The first event was a trip to Africa accompanying Secretary of State George Shultz during the last week of January. On the long transatlantic flight, I became acquainted with Assistant Secretary of State for Africa Chester Crocker and USAID administrator Peter McPherson.

The first stop was Liberia, where President Samuel Doe received Secretary Shultz within an hour of our arrival. A former army sergeant who came to power by shooting President William Tubman in 1980, Doe was in an argumentative mood. He literally shouted at Shultz that Liberia was America's best friend in Africa and yet was receiving little in return. The United States had provided significant development aid over the years, most of which had gone to waste. But to appease Doe, Administrator McPherson told Doe that he would send a team to Monrovia to develop an economic growth package.

In the evening, Doe gave a dinner in Shultz's honor. It looked like a pre–Civil War event that we all had seen in the film *Gone with the Wind.*

Shultz's next stop was Nairobi, Kenya, where he met with President Daniel Arap Moi. Kenya has always been one of the economic leaders in Africa. Shultz was pleased to see evidence of this during his visit. In his conversation with Moi, Shultz cautioned him against his tendency to undermine Kenya's fragile democracy. Moi was polite, but not particularly receptive. Shultz ended his stay with a daylong visit to the Masai Mara game park, where the animals were abundant.

In a gesture to francophone Africa, Shultz's last stop was in Cameroon. There he met with President Paul Biya in the port city of Douala, because the runway in the capital city, Yaoundé, was not long enough for Shultz's airplane. The conversation was friendly, with Biya expressing satisfaction with U.S. private investments.

The most important result of Shultz's trip to Africa had been the possible opening to economic reform in Liberia. Samuel Doe was the first indigenous, or "country," person to preside as Liberia's head of state. His predecessors had all been descendants of the original group of former American slaves who settled in Liberia in 1834. None of those heads of state had showed any interest in the economic development of the indigenous people. Samuel Doe appeared to represent a breakthrough.

In April 1986, National Security Advisor Frank Carlucci informed me that President Reagan had decided to resume normal public activity, after keeping a low profile since the Iran-Contra scandal. His first "coming out" activity would involve receiving a briefing from me on Mozambique. The president had specifically asked to be briefed on Mozambique.

The briefing was scheduled for a Monday morning at 9 a.m.

When I arrived, I was introduced to Howard Baker, Reagan's new chief of staff. It was Baker's first day on the job. Before I could begin my briefing, he asked me, "Do you have a son named Marc?" I said yes. Baker then said, "I sat next to Marc yesterday on the flight from Miami. He is a very intelligent young man." All this chit-chat about my son was going on in front of Reagan, who did not seem to mind as he waited for his briefing on Mozambique. Finally, I said to Baker, "Marc has degrees in electrical engineering from Harvard and Stanford, and he has a very good job with Booze-Allen. Did you suggest to him that it was time to get out of the house and find his own place to live?" Everyone, including Reagan, got a good laugh at that, and we then turned to Mozambique.

Reagan said that he was receiving mail from friends in Orange County, California, where he had his home. They were advising him to support an antigovernment insurgent group in Mozambique called RENAMO. They argued that the government was Marxist, while RENAMO was anti-communist and pro-West. They compared Mozambique to the other former Portuguese colony, Angola. The United States was supporting the anticommunist insurgents, UNITA, against the Marxist Angolan regime and the Cuban troops Fidel Castro had sent to Angola. Reagan's friends were saying that the Mozambique situation was the same as the one in Angola, and the president asked what I thought.

In my opinion, I said, it would be a bad idea to support REN-AMO. I expressed this view knowing full well that the State Department agreed with me. I said that the leader of RENAMO was a cruel human rights violator who forces ordinary Africans to leave their homes and fields to act as human mules to carry his equipment and who kills critics at the drop of a hat. He and his fighters seize people's homes and food. I noted that the Angolan program was starting to lose support in the Congress from liberal Democrats like Howard Wolpe and Steve Solarz, both on the Foreign Affairs Committee, and said, "Mr. President, if we start supporting a nasty guy like Alphonse Dhlakama, the head of RENAMO, we could end up losing our Angola project in support of UNITA."

President Reagan's response was interesting. He said, "OK, I will take your advice about RENAMO, but I want you to talk to the State Department about starting a peace process in Mozambique.

The RENAMO people are not men from Mars. They are Mozambicans."

I repeated the president's instruction to Assistant Secretary of State Chester Crocker, who immediately contacted Joaquim Chissano, Mozambique's president. Chissano indicated support for initiating a peace process but said that the powerful political bureau of his ruling party, FRELIMO, was totally opposed. They kept insisting that RENAMO was an artificial creation of the white-minority South African apartheid regime, which was seeking revenge for Mozambique's support for the antiapartheid fighters.

Chissano had an idea. President Reagan should invite him for an informal meeting to which he would bring some FRELIMO hardliners. Reagan was amenable to this and extended the invitation. President Chissano answered in the affirmative and arrived in Washington with his FRELIMO colleagues. After listening to President Reagan's argument, the FRELIMO leaders caved in by agreeing to negotiations with RENAMO.

Negotiations began in mid-1987. In January 1989, at the end of the Reagan administration, the Mozambican peace talks remained stalemated, and the guerrilla war continued. It was clear that the FRELIMO hardliners still hoped for a military solution.

The Mozambique issue notwithstanding, most of my time as Africa director on the NSC was spent supporting Assistant Secretary Crocker in his marathon negotiation in Angola. He had two objectives:

- Implement United Nations Resolution 435 that required the Republic of South Africa to bring its mandated territory Southwest Africa to independence.

- Organize the departure of the Cuban troops who had been present in Angola since shortly after its independence in 1975. After Portugal granted independence to Angola, the three anti-Portuguese insurgent groups began to fight among themselves for control of the new government. One of the insurgent groups, the MPLA, the Popular Movement for the Liberation of Angola, was an affiliate of the Portuguese Communist Party.

***

Crocker's challenge was twofold. First, persuade the white minority South African government to begin the transition of Southwest Africa to independence. The South African government acknowledged its responsibility under UN Resolution 435 but argued that it could not take any action as long as Cuban troops occupied the Southwest African border. Secondly, persuade the Angolan government to ask the Castro government in Cuba to bring its troops home.

But the Angolan government argued that it needed the Cuban troops to help defend against the two Angolan insurgent groups who continued the fight for power against the MPLA that had begun even before independence. These two "anti-communist" groups, UNITA and the FNLA, had support from South Africa, Zambia, and Zaire.

In March 1987, Crocker asked me to accompany him on a visit to Luanda, Angola's capital, to further negotiate the departure of the Cuban troops. It was the first of fourteen international and domestic trips that I made with Crocker between March 1987 and December 1988.

In Luanda, there was no U.S. embassy. We did not recognize the Angolan government that had power only with the protection of Castro's Cuba. The UK embassy, which had agreed to protect American interests in Angola, helped us with appointments and hotel accommodations. The Angolan officials we met were quite cordial. As a sign of their interest in Crocker's peace process, the president of the republic, Eduardo dos Santos, received us.

We also traveled to South Africa, where our main contacts were with Foreign Minister Rolof "Pik" Botha and his permanent secretary, Neil van Heerden. Both gentlemen were cordial but quite adamant. There could be no change in the status of Southwest Africa so long as Cuban troops and Southwest Africa Peoples' Organization (SWAPO) armed insurgents were roaming Angola.

The situation remained stalemated until April 1988, when I received a telephone call in my office at the NSC from Peggy Dulaney, the daughter of Citibank president David Rockefeller. She was calling from Havana, Cuba, and said she had a message from

Cuban leader Fidel Castro. The message was: "Invite the Cuban government into the negotiations, and everything will go well."

I quickly took this message to Assistant Secretary Crocker. Together, we went to see Secretary of State George Shultz. We assumed that the default reaction would be something like: "The Reagan administration will not sit at the same table as representatives of Castro's Cuba."

Secretary Shultz immediately saw that a new opportunity had opened. He expressed the view that Cuban participation in the talks could initiate a process leading to a solution. He would support Cuban participation provided the Cubans agreed not to raise any bilateral U.S.-Cuban issues. He took the proposal to President Reagan, who agreed.

As soon as the Cubans joined the talks, progress was rapid. At one point, we flew to Havana in a U.S. Air Force plane for a negotiating session After the first day of discussions, Fidel Castro joined us for dinner, where he treated us to an hourlong speech covering the entire horizon of world politics. After the third day, when we returned to the aircraft for the flight back to Washington, on each seat we found a box of Cuban cigars and a bottle of Cuban rum.

Between March and October 1988, we had several sessions in Brazzaville in the Republic of Congo, a venue especially convenient for both the Angolans and the South Africans. By the end of October, in a final session in Brazzaville, an agreement appeared:

- The Cuban troops would depart Angola over a period of eighteen months.

- South Africa would transfer control of Southwest Africa to the United Nations.

- Southwest Africa would enter a two-year transition period under UN control on the way to becoming the independent nation of Namibia.

***

One of my assignments during the talks was to brief Congo's president, Denis Sassou-Nguesso, as I was the only member of the delegation who spoke French. Not surprisingly, the president was ecstatic that this important peace agreement had been concluded in his country.

The actual agreement was signed at the UN in New York during the second week of December 1988. It was a major diplomatic triumph for Assistant Secretary Chester Crocker.

After Vice President George H. W. Bush defeated Governor Michael Dukakis in the November 1986 presidential election, I needed to find a new assignment. I decided to lobby for the position of principal deputy assistant secretary in the State Department's Bureau of African Affairs. I assumed that President-elect Bush would be recruiting a Republican political appointee to be assistant secretary.

14

ASSISTANT SECRETARY OF STATE FOR AFRICAN AFFAIRS

Shortly after he was sworn in as president on January 20, 1989, George H. W. Bush named his longtime political partner, James A. Baker III, to be his secretary of state. The following month, Baker asked to see me. He informed me that President Bush had decided to nominate me to be assistant secretary of state for Africa. With surprise and delight, I accepted immediately.

Out of curiosity, I asked Baker why Bush had not selected a Republican political person. Baker responded that Bush was unable to identify a Republican with the necessary qualifications to run the Africa Bureau.

My family and I began to plan for a formal swearing-in during the month of April 1989. It was to be the standard event presided over by the secretary of state in the Benjamin Franklin ceremonial room on the State Department's eighth floor. Before that planning could be completed, Secretary Baker called to instruct me to be sworn in immediately by the director of protocol. There was a crisis in the Sudan, and I had to fly there immediately to put out the fire.

After the UK brought the Sudan to independence in 1957, a low-grade civil war erupted. Africans living in the southern third of the Sudan engaged in armed insurgency against the Arab government in the capital city of Khartoum. The insurgency was still simmering in 1989, thirty-two years later. The immediate crisis in April 1989 was caused by the government's decision to halt all cargo traffic on the Nile River, thereby depriving the people in the south of vital food and medicine. The government had decided they could defeat the insurgents by starving the population.

I arrived in Khartoum the first week of April 1989 and met

immediately with Prime Minister Sadik el-Mahdi, along with the U.S. ambassador, Norman Anderson. I told the prime minister that although we understood his desire to defeat the insurgency, it would be unacceptable to the United States and the international community for the government to inflict great hardship on an entire population. I told him that we were available to help find a negotiated solution. El-Mahdi understood that I was speaking for President Bush. He realized he had gone too far and immediately ended the blockade.

After completing this assignment, I was able to plan a "gala" swearing-in that took place in April in the Benjamin Franklin room, with about one hundred invitees. I was pleased that my mother and brother were able to come down from New York for the event.

Getting down to work, I started brainstorming sessions with my senior colleagues in the bureau: Ambassador Jeffrey Davidow, Ambassador Irvin Hicks, Alison Rosenberg who moved with me to State from the NSC, and Ambassador John Davidson, who was head of our East Africa office. Our main concerns were the three major civil wars that were raging, in Ethiopia, Angola, and Mozambique. We concluded that we could not hope to accomplish our key policy of promoting economic development as long as these wars were impeding agriculture, creating tens of thousands of refugees and displaced persons, and discouraging private investments in entire subregions.

I took this conclusion to Secretary Baker and told him that we wanted to engage in mediation to end these wars. He responded that he fully understood our analysis, as well as our proposal. But he did not believe that these wars involved any U.S. interests. In Texas language, he said, "We ain't got no dogs in those fights." In other words, the United States should stay out. Naturally, my colleagues and I were disappointed.

Then, three months later a new player entered the picture, and everything changed. In the Soviet Union, Mikhail Gorbachev became first secretary of the Communist Party and head of state. His main objective was to end the Cold War. In July 1989 President Bush invited him to Washington, where they pledged to work together to lower tensions and to work for peaceful solutions. This new relationship was described as "détente."

About a week after Gorbachev's visit, Secretary Baker informed me that Gorbachev had asked Bush for assistance in ending the civil wars in Ethiopia and Angola. Baker explained that the Soviets were spending a billion dollars a year in each of those countries supporting the so-called Marxist governments. The Soviets could no longer afford the cost and wanted those wars to end as soon as possible. Baker informed me that President Bush had promised Gorbachev that we would become involved in efforts to end both conflicts. Baker then instructed me to explore all possibilities for helpful U.S. actions.

Shortly thereafter, I received a phone call from Anatoly Adamishin, the Soviet Foreign Ministry's director for Africa and Human Rights. He said that we needed to talk, and I agreed. Since I had never been to Moscow, I offered to visit him there. His response to my suggestion was blunt: "Do not be ridiculous. We meet in Rome."

So, we met in Rome during the last week of July. I was accompanied by East Africa Director John Davidson and my executive assistant, Robin Sanders. Adamishin recommended that I go to the Ethiopian capital, Addis Ababa, to meet with President Mengistu Haile Mariam. My mission would be to persuade him that the civil war could not be won militarily. The two insurgencies in Eritrea and Tigray could not be defeated. It was necessary to begin mediation talks with the Eritrean People's Liberation Front (EPLF) and the Tigrean Peoples Liberation Front (TPLF). Adamishin said that he would make sure that President Mengistu would receive me for a substantive discussion.

In August I went to Addis, where President Mengistu received me immediately. What struck me as I entered his office were the Jewish stars of David all over the walls and ceiling. I immediately thought of the Amhara legend about the biblical romantic relationship between King Solomon and the Queen of Sheba from today's Yemen. According to the legend, the child born of that liaison became Menelik, the first emperor of Ethiopia.

Mengistu invited me to comment about the state of the Ethiopian-U.S. relationship. I had my checklist.

First, I told him that we considered his government's human rights situation very bad, marked by extrajudicial killings of political opposition and thousands of political prisoners.

Next, I spoke about the two internal wars. The Eritrean province was in a state of armed rebellion, conducted by the Eritrean People's Liberation Front since 1962, almost three decades. In the northern province of Tigray, the Tigrayan Peoples Liberation Front launched an armed rebellion when Mengistu took power in 1972. I told Mengistu that both wars were unwinnable; the insurgents were based in the mountains, from which they mounted attacks and retreated into difficult terrain.

Then I talked about a group of roughly twenty thousand Ethiopians of the Jewish faith who wanted to emigrate to Israel but who were being blocked by the regime.

Mengistu asked for advice about ending the two internal wars. I recommended that a distinguished person be approached to act as mediator, and I suggested former president Jimmy Carter. Mengistu liked the idea and asked me to initiate the contact, which I did. Carter accepted on behalf of his foundation and began work immediately in January 1990. On their side, the TPLF accepted a mediation proposal from the Government of Italy. During both negotiations, the fighting continued in Eritrea and Tigray.

By the end of April 1990, the mediation efforts by Carter and the Italians had made no progress. In early March, we had received a message from the head of the EPLF insurgents, Isaias Afwerki, saying that the EPLF had lost confidence in President Carter. They argued that Carter was insisting on a role for the United Nations, but the EPLF said that the UN had started the problem in the first place by placing the former Italian colony of Eritrea into a federation with Ethiopia. In 1962 Ethiopian emperor Haile Selassie unilaterally abolished this federation, and the EPLF insurgency began immediately thereafter,

In early March 1990, both the EPLF and the TPLF requested that the Department of State become the official mediator. I accepted the responsibility. Shortly after I started mediation sessions in the second week of April, the military situation on the ground began to change dramatically. After decades of confining the EPLF and TPLF rebels to their mountain caves, the Ethiopian military began to fall back.

The TPLF insurgents started moving south with little opposition, capturing town after town. In Eritrea, the EPLF captured the provincial capital city of Asmara within a week. By the end of the second week of March, the TPLF was at the gates of Addis, waiting for the mediator to decide whether or not they should enter the capital.

On March 15, I was contacted by Ethiopia's acting president, Tesfaye Dinka, who requested that the TPLF be authorized to enter Addis. He was worried that the returning leaderless Ethiopian troops could cause harm to the city and its population. Our chargé d'affaires, Ambassador Robert Houdek, agreed. I told Tesfaye Dinka that I would authorize the TPLF to enter Addis only after the 18,000 Ethiopian Jews gathered in a camp outside the city could be evacuated to Israel. He agreed. I called Yuri Lubrani, the Israeli diplomat in charge of Israeli relations with Ethiopia, and within hours, Israeli aircraft were rotating between Tel Aviv and Addis. All seats were taken out of the aircraft so that each could take 500 passengers cramped together for the three-hour flight. The entire group of 18,000 were transferred to Israel within 72 hours. The TPLF entered Addis, and they effectively took control of Ethiopia, minus Eritrea. Their control of national power was to last for twenty-seven years. And we were able to assure the Soviets that Ethiopia would not be a burden to them. Angola, of course, remained a problem.

In mid-June, I asked the leaders of the TPLF, the EPLF, and the OLF to meet me in London to plan for the future of Ethiopia. (The OLF, the Oromo Liberation Front from Ethiopia's Oromia province, had played a supporting role in the insurgency.)

We met at the American Embassy. The UK Foreign Office provided logistical support, and I invited them to send an observer to the meeting.

The first thing we agreed upon was that an immediate declaration of independence by Eritrea would constitute too much of a shock to the Ethiopian nation. It had to be done gradually. We decided on a three-year transition, followed by a referendum of the Eritrean people to decide between remaining in Ethiopia or becoming a sovereign independent nation. The TPLF, which was in command in the capital city, agreed to hold an all-parties conference in July to decide on a new constitution and a transition period for democratic elections. At the last minute, the OLF head of delegation, Lencho Leta, said that the province of Oromia should also have a referendum similar to Eritrea's. I dismissed that as being too late.

After we had completed the discussions, the Ethiopians suggested that I issue a statement to the press on their behalf. I called the American Embassy and requested that they set up a press briefing. When I arrived at the appointed time the next morning, I found a packed house with lots of TV cameras.

During the briefing I mentioned that the Eritreans would have a referendum to determine if they would become independent or remain a province of Ethiopia. Unsurprisingly, this decision became the big headline.

During the question period, one journalist pointed out that the United States had consistently opposed the breaking up of African states after they had become independent. How is it possible, then, that we would be willing to accept the breaking up of Ethiopia? I responded by expressing the hope that the Eritrean people would vote to remain part of Ethiopia but pointed out that this was a special case in that the people of Eritrea, an Italian colony for fifty years, had never been accorded the right of self-determination. As the Eritrean people had never been consulted about their own political fate, they would now be consulted for the first time.

After the press conference, I went upstairs to the Political Section, where I had a visitor's office. A couple of hours later, I received a call from Secretary Baker. He had seen the reports about my press conference in the early hours of Washington and asked if it was accurate that I had said the U.S. would accept the breaking up of Ethiopia. I said that the report was accurate. The secretary responded that my remarks were about to create serious problems for him in Europe. The U.S. was trying to prevent the breakup of Yugoslavia, from which Slovenia and Croatia were on the verge of seceding. He feared that the U.S. press would seize on the contradiction: Cohen in London was accepting a possible secession of Eritrea, while Baker in Washington was trying to maintain Slovenia and Croatia inside Yugoslavia. I could tell that he was quite unhappy with me.

***

One week later, I traveled to Lisbon for the signing of the peace agreement ending the Angolan civil war, which we had an important role in resolving. There I met Baker, who represented the United States. When he saw me, he was all smiles because the American press had not picked up on the contradiction.

Our involvement in Angola began with the ceremonies celebrating the independence of Namibia in March 1990. Since the United States had played such a crucial role in that success story, Secretary Baker decided to head the U.S. delegation. Besides me, he invited my predecessor, Chester Crocker, and Edward Perkins, the U.S. ambassador to the United Nations.

The next day, Secretary Baker requested a call on the president of Angola, Eduardo Dos Santos. He had been reluctant to begin a mediation process with the UNITA rebel group, headed by Jonas Savimbi, because the United States and South Africa were both providing them with arms and money. In fact, South African troops were present in Angola actively defending the northern Namibian border against the Cuban troops.

During the conversation with Dos Santos, Baker explained that it was not the intention of the United States to overthrow his government in favor of UNITA. We were seeking a peaceful resolution to the conflict. Baker recommended that a mediator be appointed and indicated that the U.S. would be willing to lead the mediation. Dos Santos considered the U.S. unacceptable because of its support for UNITA. Baker then proposed Portugal, which Dos Santos found acceptable.

On the way back to Washington, Baker stopped in Kinshasa, the capital of Zaire (now the Democratic Republic of the Congo), to meet with President Mobutu and UNITA leader Savimbi. After listening to Baker's presentation, Savimbi accepted mediation by the Portuguese.

Baker continued on to Washington, while I went to Lisbon for consultations with the Portuguese. There I met with Deputy Foreign Minister José Barroso, who was quite happy to accept the assignment.

Barroso decided to take over a hotel training school in the

Lisbon suburb Bicesse, where the two Angolan delegations were housed and where they held meetings. Hotel trainees served them. The American embassy in Lisbon provided technical support for the mediator, mainly from the military attachés, who had expertise in cease-fires, encampment, and troop transport.

The discussions that took place between April and November 1991 showed little progress. UNITA insisted on a nationwide free and fair election. The Angolan government offered a coalition regime, with Dos Santos remaining president and Savimbi becoming vice president. Savimbi and his team all spoke African languages. As children of mixed Angolan-Portuguese marriages, Dos Santos and his team spoke only Portuguese. Savimbi believed that his native language capability would help him win a national election.

As of November 1991, the discussions at Bicesse remained deadlocked. Baker pointed out that a briefing on the status of the Portuguese negotiations was on the agenda for the upcoming meeting of Presidents Bush and Gorbachev in Houston. Baker wanted me to come to the Houston meeting to give the briefing.

In Houston, the briefing was scheduled not for the heads of state but for Secretary Baker and Foreign Minister Eduard Shevardnadze. I informed them that the discussions were deadlocked, which Shevardnadze found unacceptable. He insisted that the Russians and Americans find a solution that we would jointly present to the two sides. Pointing to me, Shevardnadze said, "You, Mr. Cohen, play the role of Savimbi. Mr. Lukalev from my staff will be Dos Santos. Go into a room, and do not come out until you have a solution."

Lukalev and I retired to a private room and hammered out a draft agreement. Start with a ceasefire, arrange for the encampment of troops, start a transition period of eighteen months, and end with an election supervised by the United Nations. Two hours later, we met with Baker and Shevardnadze, who found the agreement very good and decreed: "We meet next week in Washington to sign the agreement."

The following week, the two Angolan delegations met at the State Department in the Bureau of African Affairs conference room. Director General Jonas Savimbi led the UNITA delegation. Lopo de Nascimento, secretary general of the ruling MPLA party, led the

Angolan government delegation. After reading the document, both sides agreed. Savimbi was particularly pleased, because he was sure that he would win a free and fair popular election.

A month later, Baker and I went to Lisbon for the official signing. It was quite a heady moment. In the space of one week in April 1991, we had presided over the end of civil wars in Ethiopia and Angola, much to the satisfaction of Soviet president Gorbachev.

While in Lisbon, Baker asked me to join him for an appointment with the Portuguese prime minister. Aníbal Cavaco Silva. I was expecting the discussion to focus on the U.S. military base in the Azores. But the prime minister insisted on talking about the former Portuguese colony of Mozambique. The civil war there had become a domestic political problem in Portugal, and he was hoping that the U.S. could mediate an end to that war as well. Baker looked at me with an expression that said, "Go to it, Hank."

Getting started on a mediation effort in Mozambique was difficult. In Angola and Ethiopia, the armed rebel groups were open and available to the press and the public. In Mozambique, the leader of the rebel group RENAMO, Alphonse Dhlakama, was secretive and reluctant to appear in public. He had personal relationships with the intelligence services of South Africa and Malawi, who were providing support. In addition, the senior officials in the Mozambican ruling party, FRELIMO, believed that RENAMO was totally a creation of South African intelligence, and it was up to the international community and not the Mozambican government to deal with the civil war.

American intelligence advised me that RENAMO was a popular movement in central Mozambique, which had legitimate grievances against the government in Maputo going as far back as the Portuguese colonial regime. It was thus imperative that we make RENAMO a full partner in the peace process.

We found an opening via Robert Mugabe, president of the newly independent nation of Zimbabwe, which shares a border with Mozambique. Mugabe and Dhlakama both spoke Shona, the African dialect that straddles the border. Mugabe was able to persuade Dhlakama that he could achieve his objectives only through a peace process and that he should accept the American offer to mediate. Dhlakama agreed.

The next step was to find a host-facilitator and a venue. The American embassy in Maputo recommended that we approach St. Egidio, a Catholic lay organization based in Rome. St. Egidio had a project in Mozambique to help raise poor people out of poverty. Our colleagues at the American Embassy to the Holy See then contacted the St. Egidio people, who expressed enthusiasm for the idea. Through our embassy in Rome, we were able to find financial and technical support for the mediator from the Italian Ministry of Foreign Affairs.

The Mozambicans gathered in Rome in September 1991 and began discussions that lasted for an entire year under St. Egidio guidance. We asked Cameron Hume, deputy chief of mission at the U.S. Embassy to the Holy See, to be our observer. I visited frequently to provide advice to the St. Egidio mediators and to receive updated progress reports from Cameron Hume. (One side effect of all my visits was a major increase in my consumption of pasta.)

The parties reached a final peace agreement in September 1992. The Mozambican government promised amnesty for all fighters in RENAMO, which would become a legitimate political party eligible to participate in elections. The agreement was signed in Rome under the chairmanship of President Mugabe of Zimbabwe.

Unfortunately, I had only a short period to celebrate the Mozambique agreement when I received a telephone call from the Angolan capital city Luanda. The election resulting from the Bicesse agreement had taken place. President Dos Santos was declared the winner with 49 percent of the vote. UNITA declared the announced result to be fraudulent and refused to concede. UNITA claimed they had proof of the fraud, despite UN assurances that the election was clearly free and fair. Under Angolan law, if none of the candidates received at least 50 percent of the vote, there had to be a runoff election. This would give Savimbi a second chance.

I took the first flight to Luanda and met immediately with UNITA presidential candidate Jonas Savimbi. He produced a few vote results from a voting station that gave two minor candidates the same number of votes each. This was his proof. He said that if the result were not reversed, he would go back to war.

In my discussions with the U.S. ambassador Ed Dejarnette and with UN officials, it was clear why President Dos Santos emerged the winner. Although Savimbi was considered the most popular and was expected to win easily, he had waged a negative campaign. Circulating in battle dress, accompanied by armed guards, he carried on a threatening discourse, warning. "Anyone who frequented the black market would be punished." That was not wise, since most Angolans relied on the black market to buy necessities.

Dos Santos, on the other hand, hired a public relations firm that depicted him in the media as a family man who played football with his children, with no hint of authoritarian rule. That approach accounted for his narrow victory.

Savimbi refused the runoff, continued to insist that he had won, and expected the United States government to support his claim. For the first time in our relationship, I refused his demands. We had worked hard to assure a free and fair election, as he had demanded. Dos Santos had offered him the vice presidency, but he insisted on a new election. The United States would recognize Dos Santos's victory.

When I returned to Washington, I found the pro-Savimbi crowd incredulous. When I met with them, many refused to accept my explanation. Nevertheless, I had the support of the pro-Savimbi members of Congress. They said that Savimbi had gotten his election and had to abide by it.

Predictably, Savimbi went back to war. He had an initial advantage because he had positioned his fighters throughout Angola, while the Angolan army had more or less gone back to the barracks. It took the Angolan army several months to get back to combat readiness. The war continued for ten years, until 2002, when a sniper killed Savimbi, and UNITA collapsed.

Two additional civil wars of interest to us took place in Africa during my time as assistant secretary of state.

On October 1, 1990, President George H. W. Bush was in New York to address the United Nations General Assembly. That evening, he gave a reception for the African heads of delegation at the Waldorf-Astoria Hotel. During the reception, a State Department watch officer handed me a sheet of paper noting that about one thousand Ugandan army troops had invaded northern Rwanda.

Since the heads of state of Rwanda and Uganda were both in the room, I asked them to go off in a corner to discuss this breaking news.

After their meeting, I asked Rwandan president Habyarimana what Ugandan president Museveni had told him. He responded that Museveni claimed to know nothing about the incident. Two days later, when I met with Museveni in Washington, he gave me the same response. Those troops had gone into Rwanda without authorization, he insisted, and would be disciplined.

The real story was quite different. The Ugandan army units that had invaded Rwanda were composed of Tutsi ethnics descended from the 200,000 Tutsi refugees who had fled to Uganda in 1960. They had been subjected to pogroms by the majority Hutu ethnics who had taken power after independence from Belgium. This 1990 invasion constituted the first step in a plan by the Tutsi military leadership to take power in Rwanda. Ugandan president Museveni was aware of the project and gave it his active support. For example, he set up a military field hospital near the border to care for Tutsi wounded. The Tutsi invaders even had a name: The Rwandan Patriotic Front.

A few days later, I received a call from an officer at the U.S. Army Command and General Staff College in Fort Leavenworth, Kansas. He said that one of the students, General Paul Kagame of Uganda, had requested authorization to leave the course early to return home. Since I was financing this student, he needed my authorization to release him. I said yes.

Shortly after Kagame's return to Uganda, the Tutsi commander of the Rwandan Patriotic Front, Major General Fred Rwigyema, was mysteriously killed, shot in the back, allegedly by a sniper. Kagame became the commander of the Rwanda Patriotic Front (RPF).

I was particularly bothered by the rise of the RPF, because we had made some progress in persuading President Habyarimana to accept pluralism. He allowed the existence of opposition parties, many of them joint Hutu-Tutsi parties. Just prior to the RPF invasion, I had arranged for a representative of the U.N. High Commission for Refugees to visit Kigali for discussions about bringing the Tutsi refugees back. But the RPF invasion stopped everything. Habyarimana increased the size of his army tenfold, at great cost. As a result, the military situation became stalemated, with RPF forces occupying the northern 20 percent of Rwanda. In 1992, peace talks under UN sponsorship began in Arusha, Tanzania. When I left the Bureau of African Affairs in April 1993, talks were still underway. A year later, in April 1994, while I was assigned to the World Bank, the tragic Rwanda genocide occurred. The entire Great Lakes region was traumatized.

Another civil war that engaged the Bureau of African Affairs during my time took place in Liberia. On Christmas eve 1991, 250 armed fighters entered Liberia from neighboring Côte d'Ivoire. The leader was Charles Taylor, a former Liberian senior civil servant who had escaped to the United States in 1990. Accused of stealing money from the General Services Administration, he made his way to Massachusetts, where he hoped to escape Liberian law. The Liberian government of President Samuel Doe sent an extradition order that landed Taylor in a Massachusetts prison, but the Liberians delayed in sending the file that was to be used in court to finalize Taylor's extradition. After six weeks of inaction, Taylor "escaped" and made his way to Ghana, where he was recruited by agents of Muamar Gaddafi, the Libyan "Leader."

In Libya, Taylor underwent military training. And, with Libyan help, recruited Liberian fighters, who joined him in Côte d'Ivoire near the town of Mann. Ivoirian President Houphouët-Boigny apparently had no objection to this activity.

Immediately after the Christmas eve invasion, the Liberian army sent a company of troops to the Ivoirian border. The troops had neither the training nor the will to fight. The best they could do was destroy a Liberian village in which Taylor's fighters had spent the night.

A month after the invasion, President Doe sent a delegation to Washington headed by Winston Tubman, son of a former Liberian president, to ask for assistance. We could provide material assistance, we said, but not U.S. military forces. Meanwhile, Taylor's forces quickly reached the outskirts of the capital city, Monrovia.

The siege of Monrovia soon became a humanitarian disaster. There was no food, and the army began abusing the civilians. Our view was that Taylor could not be stopped and that it was necessary to end the terrible suffering of the civilians trapped inside Monrovia. I made the decision to evacuate President Doe to another African country and allow Taylor to take over the capital and the government.

I was due to fly to Monrovia in a U.S. Air Force C-130 aircraft to pick up President Doe and his family and take them to Togo, where they could receive asylum. Before I could depart, National Security Adviser Brent Scowcroft called to inform me that President Bush did not want me to go on this trip. In fact, he wanted the U.S. government to end its diplomatic intervention in the Liberian war. Deeply disappointed, I followed orders.

Shortly thereafter, in July 1991, the Economic Community of West African States (ECOWAS) decided to intervene. Fearing a takeover of Liberia by Gaddafi, the West Africans sent several thousand troops to Monrovia, where they engaged in combat against Taylor's forces. In view of President Bush's order, I devoted time to other priority issues. But the Africa Bureau remained in crisis mode over Liberia, mainly because of the large number of American citizens living there.

In July 1992, National Security Advisor Scowcroft called me to say that President Bush was troubled by criticism that the U.S. government was not doing anything to end the war in Liberia. After all, Liberia was an offspring of American freed slaves. The U.S. should show concern. The president wanted me to become active in Liberia again, with limitations.

I decided to do a tour of the West African region to talk about Liberia. The ECOWAS military, consisting mainly of Nigerian, Ghanaian, and Guinean troops, were preventing Charles Taylor from capturing Monrovia. On the other hand, they were not making an effort to defeat Taylor. It was a stalemate.

In Ouagadougou, Burkina Faso, I saw Libyan aircraft unloading supplies for delivery to Charles Taylor via Côte d'Ivoire. In Abidjan, Côte d'Ivoire, President Houphouët-Boigny claimed to be totally uninvolved in Liberia, although he was the main strategist for support to Charles Taylor. In discussions with several heads of state, I heard a consensus that Taylor was there to stay and that he had to be part of the solution.

During my visit to Côte d'Ivoire, U.S. ambassador Ken Brown

and I drove to the Liberian border near the Ivoirian town of Mann. We crossed into Liberia and drove about fifteen miles to Charles Taylor's camp. The first thing that struck us were about a dozen young boys, armed with machine guns, who were guarding the camp. It was frightening.

Inside the main hut, we found Charles Taylor sitting on a throne, with a photo on the wall behind him of President John F. Kennedy. He was clearly expecting to become president of Liberia. During our discussion, I asked Taylor if he would be willing to enter into negotiations with ECOWAS. He said yes. I reported this to the State Department and was quickly reprimanded for violating President Bush's order not to take charge of the problem.

Did my tour of West African nations demonstrate an interest in the Liberian tragedy? It probably did. The problem was finally solved by ECOWAS, which started talks with Taylor that led to a cease-fire, an election, and a victory by Charles Taylor. There was considerable evidence that many Liberians voted for Taylor out of fear.

In July 1992, Israeli ambassador Zalman Shoval asked to see me. This was most unusual because the Israeli embassy normally covered U.S.-African relations at a lower level. The ambassador said he had a letter for me from Prime Minister Yitzhak Rabin thanking me for helping to improve Israeli-African relations.

After the 1972 Arab-Israeli war, the Israelis had occupied Egypt's sovereign territory of the Sinai Peninsula for many years. The Egyptian government approached the African governments demanding that they break relations with Israel because Israel was occupying "African territory." Except for South Africa, Botswana, Namibia, and Malawi, the African governments complied.

Shortly after I became assistant secretary for Africa, President Bush had asked me to encourage the African governments to renew relations with Israel. Accordingly, I included this matter on my agenda during my frequent travels to Africa. By the middle of 1992, the Africans who had broken relations with Israel had renewed them. I appreciated Rabin's acknowledgement and thanks.

***

The U.S. presidential election of November 1992 had Governor Bill Clinton of Arkansas challenging incumbent George H. W. Bush. I was hoping for Bush's re-election, because I thought I could manage to be nominated for another important job. It was clear that Bush liked the way I handled the Africa job. He actually said that to my wife, Suzanne, at a White House reception.

Clinton's election changed everything. I had to think of other options. During Clinton's inauguration on January 20, 1993, Suzanne and I took a vacation in Cancún, Mexico. While there, I received two phone calls. Under Secretary for Management–designate Brian Attwood called to inform me that my successor as assistant secretary for Africa would be Ambassador George Moose, like me, a career Foreign Service officer. George was an excellent choice.

The second phone call was from Ambassador Genta Holmes, the director general of the Foreign Service, to ask if I might be interested in being nominated to be the U.S. ambassador to Haiti. I responded that I had spent most of my career in third world nations and would prefer, therefore, to go somewhere other than Haiti.

15

GLOBAL COALITION FOR AFRICA AT THE WORLD BANK

I remained assistant secretary for Africa until the Senate confirmed George Moose in April 1993. About a week later, I ran into Kim Jaycox, the World Bank vice president in charge of providing support to Africa. When I told him I was looking for a new assignment, he proposed something that I found interesting. The Bank, USAID, several other donor agencies, and about twenty African governments had formed a new informal group called the Global Coalition for Africa (GCA). The objective was to encourage the type of economic reforms that would result in an increase in private investment in Africa, both domestic and foreign. A consensus had developed that economic development could not come from development assistance alone. As in the West, development must be driven mainly by the private sector. The co-chairs of the GCA were former World Bank president Robert McNamara, Dutch Minister for International Development Jan Pronk, and President Quett Masire of Botswana. Jaycox proposed that I join the small secretariat as a senior advisor under a World Bank contract. I tentatively accepted, pending a determination about my status with the Foreign Service.

In the State Department Office of Personnel, I was told that I had two options. I could retire and begin collecting my pension. Or I could be seconded to the World Bank under a special provision for U.S. diplomats to work temporarily in United Nations agencies. I would not collect my State Department salary during the period of secondment, but I would continue to collect longevity for my eventual retirement. I opted for secondment. I was pleased to find out that the World Bank agreed to pay me the same salary as I had been receiving at the State Department.

I joined the GCA in late April 1993. The office was in the same building on K street NW along with other multilateral agencies. The director was an Ivoirien, Boubakar Aboubaker, the former secretary general of the Economic Community of West African States (ECOWAS). There were four other professionals—Aileen Marshall, a former official with the British Office of Overseas Development; Tesfaye Dinka, the former foreign minister of the Ethiopian government that was militarily forced out of power in the civil war that ended in 1991; Zayneb Lange, a World Bank officer on loan; and Mariam Coquillat, a francophone African, also from the World Bank.

Dinka and I were well acquainted, as we had worked together in 1991 to end the Ethiopian civil war "on a soft landing." Indeed, I had arranged for Dinka and his family to emigrate to the United States under the law of political asylum.

The GCA also had two international partners, the United Nations Development Program (UNDP) and the Japanese International Cooperation Agency (JICA). Both agencies cooperated closely with GCA in its various efforts to encourage African governments to adopt the right policies.

In June 1993, two months after I joined GCA, I accompanied the entire staff on a trip to Tokyo to participate in JICAD, the Japanese International Conference on African Development. Held every five years, JICAD attracted about a dozen African heads of state, as well as thirty-five development ministers. The GCA and UNDP were listed as JICAD cosponsors. During the three-day conference, the economic counselor of the American embassy told me that the Japanese government was making a special effort to engage in development efforts in Africa essentially because of public political pressure. It was expected that Japan, a relatively rich nation, would contribute to the world's poorest nations in Africa. Among the numerous speeches and social events at JICAD, the most important activity was networking, marked by informal meetings among donor country and African government representatives.

GCA had two priority activities. First, we conducted research on individual African countries. Based on the results, we wrote papers recommending the reform of economic policies that would lead to enhanced growth and poverty reduction.

Secondly, GCA organized annual meetings of donor country officials and African governments, usually in an African capital. The Benin capital, Cotonou, was one of our favorites, because the hotels were so well organized for large numbers of delegates.

The donor representatives were usually the ministers of international development. The African governments were represented by their ministers of finance, sometimes accompanied by the foreign ministers. Depending on the chosen theme of the meeting, the GCA staff prepared background papers and arranged for one donor and one African representative to speak about the issues presented. During a three-day period, besides speech-making, we spent a lot of time together in informal exchanges. The main theme, from Chairman McNamara on down, was the importance of establishing an enabling environment for private sector investments by both domestic and foreign entrepreneurs.

I became friendly with several delegates, both African and donor. Foreign Minister Merhafe of Botswana was particularly friendly and amusing. One year, there was tension between Botswana and neighboring Namibia because of disagreement over a section of their common border. On the first day of that year's GCA meeting in Cotonou, I decided to play a trick on Merhafe. I told him about a (fake) news flash that the Namibian army was attacking Botswana along the disputed border. Trusting my good American communications, he immediately went into a state of panic and grabbed his phone. Luckily, I was able to stop him from calling. From then on, he was very cautious before believing anything I said.

In 1994, my good friend and colleague Jim Woods, deputy assistant secretary of defense for Africa, retired. We decided to form a consulting firm to be known as Cohen and Woods International. Our objective was to sell services to American companies either doing business in Africa or expressing interest in doing so. Jim worked full-time for the business, while I continued with GCA. (By 1998, the consulting work had become heavy enough for me to resign from GCA and join Jim in the business.)

In 1996, President Mobutu Sese Seko of Zaire, a great friend of the United States, was overthrown by an invading army from Rwanda, consisting of both Rwandan and Zairian fighters. The Zairois, who had been living in exile in Tanzania, were opponents of Mobutu. Mobutu saw that his own army was not willing to fight, so he went into exile in Morocco with his family and close political allies. The Rwandans decided to install a longtime Zairian political dissident, Laurent Kabila, as president. Kabila had been staging guerrilla attacks against Zaire from Tanzania for several years.

The first thing Kabila did was to change the name of the country to the Democratic Republic of the Congo (DRC). He also fired all of Mobutu's ambassadors. In the United States, there was an anti-Mobutu club within the Congolese diaspora. Kabila named the president of the club, Dr. Faida Mitifu, a professor of French at Georgia State University, to be his ambassador to the United States. He named the club's vice president, André Kapanga, to be DRC's permanent representative to the United Nations in New York.

Through a mutual friend, President Kabila contacted me. He offered me a contract to train Mitifu and Kapanga in diplomacy. This contract lasted for two years, until Ambassador Mitifu requested that it be ended. She complained that she could not accept my receiving money from the Congolese government while she and her staff were not getting their salaries regularly.

In 1998, I participated in my last annual meeting of the GCA. Like the first meeting in 1990, this one took place in Maastricht, in The Netherlands. This gave the African delegations an opportunity to see Europe. Cochairperson Jan Pronk, the Dutch minister of overseas development, was the host.

The principal theme of the meeting was the role of democracy in economic development. The meeting went along smoothly until President Robert Mugabe of Zimbabwe made his presentation. He eloquently advocated for democracy, even though governance in his own country had a long way to go before it could be designated democratic.

Unfortunately, Mugabe followed his presentation on democracy by denouncing homosexuality. His concluding sentence gave us all quite a jolt: "It is absolutely abhorrent that a man will take another man and make him into a woman."

It was not long after Mugabe's remarks that the Dutch press picked up his comment about homosexuality. Before lunch, a protesting crowd had surrounded the conference center denouncing Mugabe as a bigot. The choice of The Netherlands for this meeting clearly had its negative side.

Shortly after this meeting, I informed GCA director Ahmadou Ould Abdallah that I was resigning from the GCA to pursue business consulting fulltime. He was relieved because I was already devoting half time to business activities.

16

Cohen and Woods International, Private Consultants to Business

My Defense Department colleague and friend James Woods established the consulting firm, Cohen and Woods International (CWI), in April 1994, after we had both retired from our respective federal careers. Since I had accepted an appointment as senior adviser to the Global Coalition for Africa, Jim was managing the firm on his own, with the valuable assistance of Carl Orbann, retired U.S. Navy commander. I came to the CWI office on a daily basis, after finishing at GCA.

From the start, CWI was attractive to two categories of potential clients. In view of our prior senior government positions, African heads of state saw value in our advising their ambassadors in Washington about dealing with the U.S. government. Some American private companies saw value in our advice about dealing with African governments. The fact that CWI recommended certain American companies as investors or suppliers gave African governments a sense of confidence that they were not dealing with charlatans. American companies often consulted with CWI about the risks of investing in certain African companies.

In 1995, the major American oil company Exxon Mobil made an important discovery of crude oil in the southwestern region of the central African nation Chad. While happy with the discovery, Exxon was apprehensive about the security situation in the region, centered on Doba, the regional capital. The company asked me if I would be available to brief their executives. They had seen news reports of armed militias attacking villages, as well as each other.

I agreed to do the briefing and had expected to go to Houston to give a single briefing, returning immediately to Washington. But it was more complicated than that. There were three separate companies, with three sets of executives: Exxon Inc., Exxon Chad, and Exxon International. The first two were in Houston, while Exxon International was in Morristown, New Jersey.

My advice to the executives was to go ahead with the project despite the persistent violence. I explained that the Chadians who engaged in the violence, for whatever reason, would unanimously want to see their country benefit from the oil resource. For that reason, I said, they would certainly not want to bother the exploitation of the oilfield. I also advised the company that if the fighting ever came close to the oilfield, they could shut down for a few weeks at a time for the safety of their employees.

As a result of my advice, Exxon decided to proceed with the project. A second major challenge was the requirement to build a thousand-mile pipeline to the sea, through Cameroon to the port of Kribi. And Cameroon's government insisted on being compensated for the oil flow per barrel.

There were also environmental issues. The pipeline would be going through pristine forests. Oil spills would do considerable damage to vegetation and wildlife. When the Chadian government applied to the World Bank for a loan to make an investment in the pipeline, environmental groups objected. Exxon was able to persuade the Bank that every precaution would be taken. The Bank agreed, but it insisted that the loan be on commercial terms rather than developmental. As of 2021, the Exxon oil project in Chad continued to be profitable.

As a result of that experience, Exxon came to CWI for advice on other potential projects in Africa. The only project that I advised against was a coal project in the Democratic Republic of the Congo that Exxon Mining was contemplating. In the 1990s, the DRC was not a safe place for private investors. Indeed, a major international war took place there between 1996 and 2002.

One of our business support activities that responded to an enormous need in Africa involved electricity. The New York company ContourGlobal invests worldwide in power generation. It earns revenue from the sale of power to utilities. Contour retained CWI to assist them in introducing private power to African nations. As of the year 2021, Contour had six power plant investments in Africa, one each in Togo, Senegal, and Rwanda and three in Nigeria.

The three Nigerian plants were attached to Coca-Cola Bottling, supplying electricity heat, and carbonation. The Rwanda investment is particularly interesting; the fuel involved is methane gas suspended 500 meters below the surface in Lake Kivu, between Rwanda and the Congo (Kinshasa). The company's extraction of the methane gas has the added environmental value of preventing periodic explosions in the lake, which have caused disasters to population and livestock in the past.

Because of my partner James Woods's and my extensive experience in Africa at high political and military levels, we attracted some contracts from African heads of state. These included Presidents Dos Santos of Angola, Mobutu of Zaire, Nguessou of the Republic of Congo, Chissano of Mozambique, and Traore of Mali. These heads of state expected us to persuade the United States government to look favorably upon them. That was part of our mission, but our main approach was to mentor our clients on how to become more attractive to Washington.

We also maintained extensive contacts with members of the U.S. Congress and their staffs. We played a significant role in the adoption by the Congress, during the Clinton administration, of the Africa Growth and Opportunity Act (AGOA), which gave duty-free entry to the United States of most articles manufactured in Africa.

During the year 2021, at an advanced age, I decided to sell the Cohen and Woods International consulting firm. The buyer was a longtime colleague and friend, Steve Hayes, the former president of the U.S. Corporate Council on Africa. With that sale, my attachment to Africa took the form of a daily blog, @Cohenonafrica.com. In the end, my relationship to Africa has remained permanent.

Epilogue

It was probably preordained that I would opt for a career in the international sector. Both of my parents were born in Baltic states and emigrated to the United States as adolescents in the first decade of the twentieth century. When I was growing up, I heard several languages spoken at home along with English.

In class, as early as the third grade, I was copying maps of all the continents. We were assigned to do oral reports on individual countries.

In the family, a first cousin gave me his stamp collection as he was going off to war in the U.S. Army in early 1942. My own stamp collection was limited to American issues. As I browsed through the pages of his thick album, I was amazed at the number of countries I had never even heard of. The Vatican, of all places, had the most elaborate issues.

In high school, I always found the analyses of foreign countries and their governments to be the most interesting. In college, my professor of comparative European governments, Bernard E. Brown, thought I would be a good candidate for the Foreign Service and encouraged me to take the Foreign Service examination. He wanted to see more students from the City College of New York serving as American diplomats.

In foreign capitals, especially in those countries that have diplomatic relations with the United States, the resident American communities cover a wide range of activities beyond official diplomacy, including business, religion, education, and the multilateral development agencies. In all cases, the American embassy serves as the central hub for the entire community. American embassies also command respect among the local intellectual classes, who like to compare notes with embassy officers. For example, when I headed the Political Section in our Paris embassy, 1974–1977, heads of major French companies and French journalists were regular callers. I was particularly impressed by the occasional visits from the French head of the I.B.M. corporation in Paris. Though he had his own view of the unfolding French political situation, he also wanted to know the American perspective.

Looking back at my overall experience overseas, I remember constantly asking questions. For the most part, I found my foreign contacts willing to engage in dialogue. They were just as interested in influencing me as I was in influencing them.

Maintaining normal family life in the Foreign Service is a major challenge, especially regarding education. For that reason, I have great respect for the State Department Office of Overseas Schools, which provides fabulous support. Medical support for Foreign Service families is another real challenge. In many countries, local medical services are equal to those in America. But in other countries, the department assigns American doctors and nurses, often on a regional basis. During my ambassadorship in Dakar, Senegal, our resident American doctor served four other embassies on a rotating basis.

Modern telecommunications have made a big difference in Foreign Service life. Contacts with family in the States, especially with children in universities or boarding schools, have become a lot easier than in the past. When my family and I were in Zambia, 1965–1966, a telephone call home to my parents in New York required an advance reservation and an immediate cash payment to a post office clerk afterward. A ten-minute call with my parents cost about $100 at the time.

Do I recommend a career in the international arena to young persons today? The answer is emphatically "yes." There remain many challenges and surprises out there, and they yield much satisfaction.

INDEX

Note: Pages in *italics* refer to illustrative matter.

www.ingramcontent.com/pod-product-compliance
Lightning Source LLC
Chambersburg PA
CBHW070924270326
41927CB00011B/2718